STACK
PRESENTS

BASKETBALL
TRAINING

FOR THE ATHLETE,
BY THE ATHLETE

TRIUMPH
BOOKS

This book is available in quantity at special discounts for your group or organization.
For further information, contact:
Triumph Books
542 South Dearborn Street
Suite 750
Chicago, Illinois 60605
(312) 939–3330
Fax (312) 663–3557
www.triumphbooks.com

Printed in India
ISBN: 978-1-60078-281-7

Design, page production, and editing: Red Line Editorial

Contributing Writers:
Chad Zimmerman
Josh Staph
Chip Smith
Scott Mackar
Zac Clark
Matt Siracusa
Kyle Woody

Photos courtesy STACK Media unless otherwise indicated.

ABOUT STACK

STACK is the nation's leading producer and distributor of sports performance, training, and lifestyle content for high school and college athletes and the high school sports community. Founded by Nick Palazzo and Chad Zimmerman, two former collegiate football athletes, STACK has the singular goal of improving the lives of athletes by providing safe and effective advice on how to properly boost performance without the use of steroids or other illegal performance enhancing drugs.

The name STACK stands for the complete "stack" of information an athlete needs to be more successful in all aspects of life. Key components are STACK's information, instruction, and advice on training and nutrition, which help athletes improve their physical being and performance. But STACK also addresses important life skills and teaches lessons in areas such as team building, goal setting, mental preparation, and overcoming adversity. Finally, a very important part of STACK's content mix is material related to college selection and the recruiting process, including tips and advice on character building, presenting oneself properly to coaches, and focusing on strong academics.

STACK's content does not come from individuals who claim to be "experts," but have little experience working with elite athletes. On the contrary, the information and advice provided by STACK comes directly from today's best athletes and the experts who work with them on a regular basis. Athletes such as Peyton Manning, LeBron James, Johan Santana, LaDainian Tomlinson, Allen Iverson, and Tim Duncan have willingly made their training, nutrition, or personal experiences available to STACK's audience. Why? Because they want to support STACK's mission of helping athletes safely improve their performance. By using star professional athletes as role models, STACK produces content that's real, raw, and authentic and makes a powerful, lasting impression on its readers and viewers.

CONTENTS

INTRODUCTION

How is this Book Different?

This book is a compilation of the best basketball workouts published in *STACK* Magazine since the company was launched in 2005. Over the past four and a half years, STACK content directors have observed hundreds of workouts by some of the best professional and collegiate players and strength coaches in the business. In the following pages, you'll gain exclusive insights into how successful pros such as Dwight Howard, Brandon Roy, Amar'e Stoudemire, Chris Paul, and Kevin Durant prepare their bodies to perform at peak levels during the long and demanding NBA season. Unlike those in some other publications, these workouts are real. They are the exact regimens used by each featured NBA star every day, week, month, and year. The impeccable, polished product you see on the court is crafted—with little or no fanfare—in the gym and weight room. If you want to know how these men were shaped into formidable athletes, read on.

What is STACK?

STACK is the nation's leading producer and distributor of sports performance, training, and lifestyle content for active sports participants.

Recognizing the need and in response to the demand for state-of-the-art sports performance information, former collegiate football players Nick Palazzo and Chad Zimmerman launched STACK in February 2005. Their singular goal was to improve the lives of young athletes by providing safe and effective advice on how to boost performance without the use of steroids or other illegal performance enhancing drugs. Since the company's founding, the STACK editorial team, which produces all of the company's original content, has been forging relationships with the best and brightest in the sports performance, sports nutrition, strength and conditioning, recruiting, sports psychology, and related fields, all of which are vital to developing a well-rounded athlete. Via recorded interviews and video shoots, more than 400 experts have contributed to STACK's content library, providing readers and website visitors with easy access to the cutting-edge and groundbreaking techniques that help already-elite athletes get even better. This access is what separates STACK from other media properties and what makes STACK's content real, raw, and authentic.

STACK's Objectives

The three pillars of STACK's mission to athletes are to provide:

- Information, instruction, and advice on training and nutrition, which help athletes enhance physical well-being, improve on-field performance, and avoid injury
- Emphasis on important life skills, which teach lessons in areas such as team building, goal setting, mental preparation, and overcoming adversity

- Advice on the college selection and recruiting process, including tips and suggestions on character building, presenting oneself properly to coaches, and focusing on strong academics.

STACK Platforms

STACK reaches its ever-expanding audience through STACK Media, *STACK* Magazine, STACK.com, STACK TV, and MySTACK.

STACK Media is one of the top sports properties on the Internet, with an average of 4 million unique visitors and 100 million page views per month, according to comScore. Recognizing that active young males are hard to reach online, STACK Media combines its unique and appealing editorial content with product and service offerings from a number of related partner sites to fully engage its audience through a distributed media network. From its origins as a magazine publisher, STACK Media has become the acknowledged leader in reaching active sports participants online.

STACK Magazine, requested by more than 9,000 high school athletic directors, has a circulation of 800,000 and a readership of nearly 5 million high school athletes. In keeping with the company's mission, the magazine is devoted to helping shape well-rounded athletes. Published six times throughout the school year, the magazine is loaded with expert advice from top professional athletes and their trainers. *STACK* Magazine teaches young athletes the proper way to train, eat, and develop their skills, while also educating them on how to be good teammates, respect their opponents, and handle adversity—lessons based on the experiences of pro and college athletes who have reached the pinnacle of success in their sports.

STACK.com, the digital home for all STACK content and web-based tools, provides content exclusively for youth sports participants. With coverage of more than 20 sports, and content featuring lifestyle information as well as training, nutrition, and sports skills, the site offers something for everyone with an interest in sports performance.

STACK TV, an online platform with eight channels and several categories of unique, proprietary videos, constitutes the largest video library of sports performance content on the Web. More than 4,000 [and counting] videos feature top professional and collegiate athletes, coaches, trainers, and sports nutritionists, all offering the benefits of their expertise to young athletes seeking to improve their performance.

MySTACK is a social network and recruiting site that allows athletes to create profiles with their personal information and athletic stats, upload highlight films and photos, and send their profiles to college coaches. Tens of thousands of athletes have signed up as MySTACK members, and many use the network to connect [and compete] with each other as well as to take control of the recruiting process, confirming the proposition that competition breeds success.

STACK EXPERTS

JOE ABUNASSAR
Impact Basketball
Founder and president
impactbball.com

Joe Abunassar is the former director of basketball for IMG Academies in Bradenton, Florida. He subsequently founded Impact Basketball, which has three world-class training facilities—in Bradenton, Las Vegas, and Reseda, California. Abunassar has helped his star-studded clientele attain mind-boggling success, including Olympic gold medals, NBA MVP Awards, NBA All-Stars, Collegiate All-Americans, McDonald's All-Americans, NBA Draft lottery selections, and high school all-league selections. He has trained Kevin Garnett, Chauncey Billups, Dwight Howard, Chris Bosh, Paul Pierce, Vince Carter, Danny Granger, and Mo Williams.

TRAVELLE GAINES
Elite Athletics
Director, pro athlete development
eliteathletics.com

Travelle Gaines heads up day-to-day operations and training at the recently opened Elite Athletics in Westlake Village, California. Gaines has trained numerous NFL and NBA players. Prior to his current position, Gaines worked with the Jacksonville Jaguars' strength and conditioning staff during training camp, and was a strength and conditioning coach at University of Louisiana-Monroe and Louisiana State University, training first-round picks Joseph Addai, JaMarcus Russell, Glenn Dorsey, LaRon Landry, Dwayne Bowe, and Craig "Buster" Davis.

STEVE HESS
Denver Nuggets
Strength and conditioning coach
nuggets.com

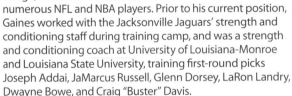

Steve Hess oversees and develops all aspects of the Denver Nuggets' strength and conditioning program, including weight training, fitness, stretching, and nutrition. He designed both the team's training facilities at the new Pepsi Center and certain functional training equipment specifically for the Nuggets. A spokesman for Eating for Life and Makoto Sports Arena, he's been featured on *NBA Inside Stuff* and on The Eating Network. He also has his own workout segment on the Altitude Sports and Entertainment Network. A part owner of FORZA Fitness in Denver, Hess sits on Under Armour's Performance Training Council whose mission, according to Hess, is "to revolutionize how athletes train."

JOE ROGOWSKI
Orlando Magic
Athletic development specialist
orlandomagic.com

Since 2006, Joe Rogowski has served as the Magic's athletic development specialist, overseeing all aspects of the team's strength and conditioning program. He joined the team in 2001 as a strength and conditioning intern. Rogowski, who is a certified member of the National Athletic Trainers Association and the National Strength and Conditioning Association, earned his bachelor's in sports medicine and athletic training from DePauw University, where he was also a standout defensive back for the Tigers' football team. He earned his master's in exercise physiology from the University of Central Florida.

ERIK PHILLIPS
Phoenix Suns
Head strength and conditioning
   coach, assistant athletic trainer
phoenixsuns.com
SportXcel
Executive VP of product research
   and development
sportxcel.com

Erik Phillips has been the Phoenix Suns' head strength and conditioning coach and assistant athletic trainer since 2005. Prior to that, he spent six years with the Denver Nuggets—the last five as assistant athletic trainer and practice facility manager. A member of the National Athletic Trainers Association, the Arizona Athletic Trainers Association, and the National Academy of Sports Medicine, Phillips is certified as a Performance Enhancement Specialist. He recently helped open the SportXcel Performance Facility in Denver, Colorado, which focuses on developing all kinds of athletes, from young superstars to weekend warriors.

JACK MANSON
New Orleans Hornets
Strength and conditioning trainer
hornets.com

As the New Orleans Hornets' strength and core trainer for the past six years, Jack Manson is responsible for designing and implementing strength and conditioning programs to help players achieve and maintain optimal performance throughout the season. He also consults with players regarding various injuries that occur during the season. Manson has practiced internal and primary care medicine, emergency medicine, and occupational medicine at

Howard University, Washington, D.C. Hospital Center, and Ochsner Clinic in New Orleans. A native of Washington, D.C., Manson received a bachelor's in physician assistantship from Howard University in 1986, and a master's in exercise physiology from Miami University [Ohio] in 1992.

SCOTT COCHRAN

New Orleans Hornets
Former assistant strength and conditioning coach
hornets.com
University of Alabama
Head football strength and conditioning coach
rolltide.com

Scott Cochran spent three seasons as assistant strength coach for the New Orleans Hornets before joining the University of Alabama in 2007 as head football strength and conditioning coach. With the Hornets, his duties included assisting with strength and conditioning programs to help players achieve and maintain optimal performance throughout the season. Earlier in his career, Cochran served as an assistant strength coach for football at his alma mater, Louisiana State University, during the Tigers' 2003 national championship run. Cochran received his bachelor's in kinesiology in 2001, and his master's in sports management in 2003, both from LSU.

ALAN STEIN

Montrose Christian School
Head strength and conditioning
   coach
montrosechristian.org
Stronger Team
Owner
strongerteam.com

Alan Stein is the head strength and conditioning coach for the nationally ranked Montrose Christian basketball team in Rockville, Maryland. He has served as the head conditioning coach for the Jordan Classic All-American team and the McDonald's All-American game. He's also a Nike Basketball performance consultant and a member of the SPARQ Trainer Network. Through his M.V.P. Vertical Jump Program, Stein shares his training expertise with high school, college, and NBA athletes, including Oklahoma City Thunder guard/forward Kevin Durant and Miami Heat forward Michael Beasley.

TODD WRIGHT

University of Texas
Strength and conditioning coach,
   men's basketball
texassports.com

Todd Wright conditioned the Clemson Tigers before taking the reins in Austin. Over the past decade he's played a major role in helping the Longhorns achieve success on the hardwood. Under his direction, Texas alums T. J. Ford [Indiana Pacers, guard] and Kevin Durant [Oklahoma City Thunder, guard/forward] garnered National Player of the Year honors in 2003 and 2007, respectively. Wright is a certified strength and conditioning specialist and is a member of the National Strength and Conditioning Association.

DWIGHT DAUB, MS, CSCS, PES, CES

Oklahoma City Thunder
Director of athletic performance,
   assistant coach
nba.com/thunder

Dwight Daub has shared his strength and conditioning expertise at every level—from junior high school to the pros. After earning his master's in exercise sports science from Eastern Illinois, Daub became a certified strength and conditioning specialist. He served as assistant S+C coach at the University of Arizona, co-head strength coach at the University of Illinois, and strength coach at the University of Utah. In 1997, he joined the Seattle Sonics as the team's strength coach and was later promoted to director of athletic performance and assistant coach.

SHAWN WINDLE

Indiana Pacers
Head strength and conditioning coach
indianapacers.com

In 2005, Shawn Windle joined the Pacers as head strength and conditioning coach and assistant athletic trainer, responsible for all aspects of the players' training and physical development. Prior to that, he served for four years as head strength and conditioning coach at Rutgers University, where he was in charge of the men's and women's basketball programs as well as all Olympic sports. A graduate of the University of Maine at Presque Isle, he earned his bachelor's in athletic training while playing varsity basketball. Windle is an NSCA Certified Strength and Conditioning Specialist, NATA Certified Athletic Trainer, and USA Weightlifting Level I Club Coach.

CHAPTER 1

CHAUNCEY BILLUPS

WITH KEVIN GARNETT

EDITOR'S NOTE

During the 2008-09 season, his 12th in the NBA, Chauncey Billups returned to his hometown of Denver and proceeded to post the second highest scoring average of his career [17.9 points per game] while handing out an impressive 6.4 assists per contest. Longtime Denver fans recognize that the Nuggets were a completely different squad with Billups leading the charge.

Before making his game-changing impact in Denver, Billups ran the show for seven seasons in Motown as the Pistons' All-Star point guard. After joining the club before the 2002–03 season, Billups led them to the 2004 NBA Championship, collecting the Finals MVP Award in the process.

After being named the NBA's Defensive Player of the Year, Kevin Garnett led the Boston Celtics to the 2008 NBA Championship. He fell just short of averaging a double-double, netting 18.8 points and 9.2 rebounds during the campaign.

Prior to his winning ways in Beantown, Garnett was the bright spot on a mostly dismal Minnesota Timberwolves squad for 12 seasons. Despite being surrounded by lesser talent for most of his career, Garnett is a 12-time All-Star and four-time All-NBA First Team selection.

CHAUNCEY BILLUPS DRIVES TO THE BASKET AGAINST THE BOSTON CELTICS. A COMBINATION OF STRENGTH TRAINING, CONDITIONING, AND BASKETBALL WORK HELPS HIM PREPARE FOR EACH SEASON.

Both Billups and Garnett have won NBA titles and dozens of awards, and both naturally assume the leadership role on highly successful teams. But the strongest link between the two is Joe Abunassar, president and founder of Impact Basketball. Abunassar has trained both studs in the off-season for most of their careers, helping them reach their highest potential with workouts that combine strength training, conditioning, and real basketball work.

In 2005, when we became aware of the opportunity to feature the training methods of one of basketball's top performance coaches and speak with two of the sport's best players in the bargain, no discussion was necessary before we accepted.

This is an updated version of the Chauncey Billups and Kevin Garnett cover feature as it originally ran in the December 2005 issue of *STACK* Magazine.

THE MOST VALUABLE PROGRAM

What I love about Joe's program is that it's completely balanced. He mixes strength training, which benefits my conditioning, with a lot of basketball stuff to improve my game on the court. Joe's program was the first to combine the two consistently. – Kevin Garnett

Garnett isn't talking about your average Joe. He's referring to Joe Abunassar, the former director of IMG Basketball Academy in Bradenton, Florida, whose client list includes Garnett, Chauncey Billups, Tayshaun Prince, Al Harrington, and Sebastian Telfair. As evidenced by their physiques and skill, training comes first with these ballers when they visit the Sunshine State.

Abunassar presides over a training world to which every elite athlete should be exposed. "There were plenty of guys I could train with just to get in shape," Billups says. "But I needed to find a person who knows about nutrition too. And Joe taught me how to eat right—when to eat, what stuff I need for my body and when I need it."

Garnett adds: "I can't lie. It's helped me; it's helped my game; it's helped me mentally; and it's helped me physically to endure the pounding of an 82-plus game season. Everything is about results. You don't do something unless you get results, and Joe gets results. Look at me and all the other guys he trains. We're doing our thing, getting it done on the court."

The secret to Abunassar's success lies in the six elements of his program: strength, performance, nutrition, corrective work/flexibility, on-court work, and recovery. He changes the intensity of each element according to the time of year to create perfect basketball periodization. Abunassar customizes each player's program to meet his specific needs. "Basketball coaches have put together great on-

court improvement programs, and strength and conditioning coaches have designed hundreds of programs to improve players in their area of expertise," Abunassar says. "Yet very few players receive instruction on properly combining these two areas with nutrition, corrective work, and effective recovery methods."

"It's totally different," Billups says. "In the league, having a trainer like Joe, you find out how much you really love the game. You do so much work that sometimes you're just like, 'Why am I doing this? … Are you serious?' So you find out how much you love it."

Here, Abunassar provides a plan with sample training sessions based on the elements and fundamentals he uses with Garnett, Billups, and his other clients. The plan is appropriate for basketball players of all ages and abilities.

1) Strength Training

"My approach to weight training is simple," Abunassar says. "I build the program from the court, backwards."

When designing a customized weight-training program, Abunassar first targets a player's on-court weaknesses. For example, if a guy is slow off the dribble, he prescribes lifts that strengthen the guy's quads, hamstrings, and glutes.

Correcting on-court weaknesses, however, is not the sole focus. Abunassar's clients' strength programs, including Garnett's and Billups', "focus on balance and improvements in overall kinetic chain function [the transfer of energy from one body part to another]." Another priority is general strength training, although Abunassar warns that too much of this can result in debilitating on-court problems.

© AP Images

"Intensity levels, specific exercises, rep/rest patterns, and ratios change depending on the time of year," Abunassar says. Whereas maintaining weight is the focus in-season, Abunassar emphasizes strength gains in the off-season. He employs three effort or intensity levels, each appropriate for the time period. These are appropriate for an athlete of any level.

Effort Level 3 – Off-season

Perform 3 sets of 10 reps for each exercise 3 days per week. The first 2 sets should be very challenging, and the third difficult to finish.

Effort Level 2 – Preseason

Perform 3 sets of 8 reps in a circuit format 3 days per week. Perform 1 set for each lift, then move to the next exercise. After completing 1 set of each exercise, move through the complete circuit 2 more times.

Effort Level 1 – In-season

Perform 3 sets of 8 reps in a circuit format 2 days per week. All lower body lifts should be replaced with corrective work.

2) Performance Training

Performance training addresses speed, agility, quickness, explosiveness, jumping ability, basketball-specific movement patterns, cardiovascular capacity, and flexibility. Improving all of these elements helps eliminate specific physical deficiencies and convert pure strength gains developed in the weight room into basketball-specific strength.

On-court training sessions include all eight performance components, making it Abunassar's preferred performance training method for basketball players. These sessions train basketball-specific movements relevant to the game.

Development of the eight performance components results from strict adherence to the prescribed on-court intensity levels. Even in the off-season, during the period of lowest on-court training intensity, performance training should still be included in the total training plan.

3) Nutrition

Being aware of what to eat and when to eat helps you:

- Store the maximum amount of energy in your body
- Use stored energy more efficiently
- Recover quickly from high intensity workouts or competition
- Avoid multiple days of poor training from fatigue and lack of body awareness
- To make sure you get enough calories and nutrients during the season, analyze your carb, protein, fat, and vitamin intake in three-day periods.

Carbohydrate Info

Carbs fuel working muscles, so increase your in-season intake—especially in the days and hours before games and training sessions.

Daily carb intake should equal about four to four and a half grams per pound of body weight.

Food eaten 30 minutes before a one-hour training session should have a higher concentration of simple sugars to provide a large amount of energy quickly.

Food eaten two hours before a two-hour game or training session should have a higher concentration of complex carbs to provide lasting energy at a slower rate.

Eating carbs within an hour after competing or training helps the body recover within 24 hours, versus up to 72 hours otherwise.

Protein Info

Protein helps the body produce enzymes used by the aerobic system to burn carbs and fat.

Daily protein intake should equal about .9 to 1 gram per pound of body weight.

Good sources of protein include chicken, fish, pork, low-fat or lean beef, eggs, low-fat dairy products, any type of bean, and nuts and seeds [though high in fat and not as protein-rich].

Fat Info

For a fit athlete, fat is an efficient energy source when carbs are simultaneously burned.

Monounsaturated and polyunsaturated fats in nuts, avocados, olive oil, and fish are beneficial to energy burning and overall health.

Limit fat in meals eaten before a high-intensity game or training session.

Vitamins and Minerals

Vitamins and minerals prevent deficiencies that can harm performance.

Antioxidants neutralize free radicals that result from high activity levels and that can damage cells.

Following is a sample eating plan that provides guidelines for meal timing and content based on practice and game schedules.

Monday: No game, practice at 11 a.m.

General Recommendation: Start hydrating early. Entering practice even a bit dehydrated affects performance and makes recovering for Tuesday's game more difficult. Drink water most of the day, but have one sports drink within 30 minutes of practice.

Breakfast: Two hours before practice, eat a low-fat, high-carb breakfast. The goal is to build muscle energy stores with complex carbs for Tuesday's game.

Recommended Foods: Non-sugar cereal, oatmeal, eggs, extra-lean bacon, lean turkey bacon, glass of fruit juice.

Recommended Supplement: Multivitamin.

Post-practice meal: This might be the most important meal of the day, because it replaces lost energy and helps the body recover for Tuesday's game. Eat carbs within 60 minutes after practice along with a balanced portion of protein, fat, and vitamins.

Recommended Foods: Chicken sandwich, turkey sandwich, burrito, pasta, rice, vegetables, baked chips, low-fat yogurt.

Recommended Supplement: Post-workout recovery shake.

Dinner: Should be of moderate caloric intake that will top off muscle energy stores.

Recommended Foods: Pasta with chicken, whole grain rice with sauce or chicken, grilled chicken, pork or fish with vegetable and side of pasta or rice, side of potatoes prepared any way but fried, one glass of fruit juice, and ample water.

Tuesday: No practice, game at 7:30 p.m.

General Recommendation: Eat lighter meals; you should be slowly building energy stores from the morning until game time. Sip water all day to recover from Monday's training and prepare for fluids lost during the game. Don't drink sports drinks until right before the game.

Breakfast: Make sure to get enough complex carbs, protein, and vitamins. The goal is to boost muscle energy stores for the game.

Recommended Foods: Eggs, waffles, whole grain pancakes, oatmeal, lean meat, fruit.

Recommended Supplement: Multivitamin.

Lunch: Use Monday's post-practice menu options for a light lunch.

Pre-game meal: Eat a light pre-game meal between 3:30 and 5:00. About 70 percent of the meal should consist of carbohydrates; the balance should be a lean protein. Avoid beef because of its high fat content and fruit because of its high sugar content. Drink plenty of water.

Recommended Foods: Pasta, rice, potatoes, chicken, fish, pork.

Post-game meal: Eat a meal within 60 minutes after the game to replace lost energy and fluids and to provide protein to repair damaged muscle cells.

Recommended Foods: Pasta with some sort of protein, rice, chicken, fish, lean meat, vegetable source for vitamin content.

Recommended Supplement: Recovery drink or shake.

4) Corrective Work/Flexibility

Poor ankle flexibility can result from knee problems. Poor hip mobility can prevent a player from moving quickly. Corrective work aims to fix and prevent these types of kinetic chain reactions. Like the rest of Abunassar's program, corrective work is customized to a player's individual needs. A physical therapist evaluating a player can identify the areas of his kinetic chain that require improvement, and then prescribe corrective flexibility training, strengthening drills, self-myofascial release exercises, and movement pattern drills. Performing the exercises daily for an extended period is the only way to correct problems. Consistency is key!

5) On-Court Training

"While all aspects of the training program are critical to producing an elite basketball player, nothing supersedes on-court drilling," Abunassar says. Because on-court workouts are customized to meet a player's long-term goals, the goals of each individual session dictate the intensity.

Abunassar points out five keys to a successful on-court training session:

1. **Go into each session fully recovered from previous workouts.** "Many coaches put players through high-intensity drill work 12 months a year. This increases risk for injury and minimizes the training's effectiveness."

2. **Separate individual on-court work from team training.** "Players have to work on improving their overall skills, not just their role within an offensive scheme."

3. **Repetition of each drill is critical.**

4. **Don't stop mid-drill to correct a problem.** "Athletes need to move through the drills and learn to self-correct during the play."

5. **Identify specific fundamental problems before the workout, then use them as improvement goals for the session.**

Abunassar's keys to building an effective training program:

1. Early in the off-season, on-court workouts should be less intense and geared toward building endurance and improving fundamentals.

2. Intervals of varied intensity during a single training session help players reach game heart rates for sustained periods of time. The length and intensity of each interval should increase as the season approaches.

3. Players cannot drill hard for five or six days a week. Recovery helps the athlete achieve maximum results.

4. Conditioning drills should be part of court work—especially as the season approaches in EL 3.

Intervals fall into three energy levels (ELs), based on target heart rates:
EL 1 = 120-136 beats per minute [bpm]
EL 2 = 137-164 bpm
EL 3 = 165-180 bpm

6) Recovery

As simple as it sounds, the body needs recovery time to absorb improvements made during training. Although Abunassar's training program uses different intensity levels, recovery prevents overtraining and maintains the program's effectiveness.

For a basketball player, recovery does not mean taking a day off. It's a combination of controlling effort levels, hydrating properly, completing corrective work, resting, and active recovery. Examples of active recovery include riding a bike, swimming, pool jogging, stretching, and light shooting.

Nutrition is also crucial to recovery. Ingesting high-carb foods within an hour after training accelerates recovery; hydration replenishes fluids lost during hard training.

During an EL 3 on-court session, a player must fully recover from the workout so he is not fatigued the next day or later in the week. When he is tired midweek, positive training gains are lost, injury is a risk, and time spent becomes time wasted.

Following is a sample plan that combines varying intensity levels, corrective work, rest, and active recovery.

Sunday/Rest Day
Monday/Intense Day:
Warm up, lift, core, and balance
High intensity court work
Play
Tuesday/Moderate Day:
Warm-up, lower body core, and balance
30-minutes high intensity court work
30-minutes light shooting
Play
Massage
Wednesday/Intense Day:
Warm-up, lift, core, and balance
High-intensity interval, court work
Play
Stretch
Thursday/Intense Day:
Warm-up, core, and balance
Court work—short intervals
Play
Massage
Friday/Active Basketball Recovery:
Warm-up, lift, core, and balance therapy
Active recovery shooting on court
Afternoon off
Saturday/Intense Day:
Warm-up
On-court work only

STRENGTH TRAINING

SINGLE-LEG DUMBBELL SQUAT

Abunassar: "You get all the benefits of a regular squat—like working the glutes, hamstrings, and quads—but you also work balance, stability, and flexibility in the leg you're using. You also work your core by forcing it to balance your body on one leg."

- Hold dumbbell in each hand with back foot on bench

- Squat down by sitting hips back

- Drive up when thigh is parallel to ground; repeat for specified reps

- Perform on opposite leg for specified reps

COACHING POINTS

➡ **Maintain tight core and keep shoulders up** ➡ **Keep knee behind toes** ➡ **Keep back flat and chest up**

SINGLE-LEG ROMANIAN DEADLIFT

Abunassar: "This lift really works glute and hamstring strength and endurance, depending on the rep scheme. The single-leg aspect emphasizes core strength and balance stability."

- Assume single-leg stance, holding dumbbell in opposite hand of working leg

- Keeping back flat, bend forward with control by shifting hips back

- Lower as far as possible, then return to standing position through same motion; repeat for specified reps

- Perform on opposite leg for specified reps

COACHING POINTS

➡ **Keep back flat** ➡ **Do not change flex in knee throughout entire motion**
➡ **Go through full range of motion**

STANDING SINGLE-ARM CABLE CHEST PRESS

Abunassar: "Standing with a cable, rather than lying on a bench, introduces rotational force. You get the same chest work while stabilizing your core and working on balance."

- With weight stack behind you, assume staggered stance and hold handle set at shoulder level

- Drive arm forward until straight

- Slowly return to starting position; repeat for specified reps

- Perform with opposite arm for specified reps

COACHING POINTS

- ➡ Keep core tight throughout exercise
- ➡ Engage chest on both push and release of cable
- ➡ Go through full range of motion

4 STANDING SINGLE-ARM CABLE ROW

Abunassar: "When you do a seated row, your body is locked into place and doesn't have to maintain balance, which is why I have the athlete stand up. It works endurance and stability of the entire body rather than just strength, so we do it when we get in season."

• With weight stack behind you, assume staggered stance and hold handle set at shoulder level

• Drive arm forward until straight

• Slowly return to starting position; repeat for specified reps

• Perform with opposite arm for specified reps

COACHING POINTS

➡ Keep core tight and body balanced throughout exercise ➡ Engage back on every rep
➡ Keep head and chest up ➡ Go through full range of motion

5 PHYSIOBALL BRIDGE HOLDS WITH WEIGHT [45-SECOND HOLD]

Abunassar: "This trains the glutes and upper hamstrings, which is where a basketball player gets most of his power. Movements should be initiated by firing the glutes, but many young guys lean forward to jump, using their quads instead. We train them how to fire their glutes in the weight room so they can do it on the court."

• Assume bridge position with shoulders on ball, feet pointed straight ahead and weight plate on stomach

• Hold bridge position for 45 seconds

• Lower; repeat for specified reps

COACHING POINTS

➡ Create straight line from shoulders to knees to engage glutes ➡ Do not allow hips to dip during hold
➡ Increase time of hold as strength increases

6 REVERSE GRIP PULLDOWN

Abunassar: "This works your lats and other muscles in the upper back. We use it more in the off-season when we are trying to build strength in those areas."

- Assume position on pulldown machine and grasp handles with palms facing body

- Pull weight down until handles are at chest level

- Control weight up until arms are completely straight

- Repeat for specified reps

COACHING POINTS

- ➡ Keep chest and head up and back flat
- ➡ Avoid using body for momentum
- ➡ Go through full range of motion

7 PHYSIOBALL WEIGHTED SIT-UP

Abunassar: "On a physioball, you have to contract the abs up and down and in an additional plane of movement. You have to balance on the ball, which recruits more muscles than lying on the ground."

- Hold weight overhead and place lower back on physioball

- Perform sit-up

- Lower with control; repeat for specified reps

COACHING POINTS

➡ Don't let ball move during sit-up ➡ Hold plate overhead by fully extending arms
➡ Hold sides of plate ➡ Go through full range of motion

8 SINGLE-LEG V-UPS

Abunassar: "This really hits your lower and upper abs simultaneously, because you raise your legs and upper body. You work your obliques as you rotate up."

- Lie on ground with arms fully extended overhead and legs straight

- Keeping arms and working leg straight, fold at waist bringing opposite arm to opposite leg

- Lower to start position; repeat for specified reps

COACHING POINTS

➡ Avoid using body for momentum
➡ Try to touch fingers to toes at top of movement
➡ Perform with control

9 ALTERNATE ARM/LEG SUPERMANS

Abunassar: "This is a great movement to strengthen most of your back muscles. Whenever you train your abs, you want to work your lower back equally to balance strength in your core."

- Lie on stomach with arms overhead and legs straight

- Raise opposite arm and leg, keeping them straight

- Lower to start position; perform on opposite leg and arm

- Repeat for specified reps

COACHING POINTS

➡ **Keep arms and legs as straight as possible** ➡ **Raise arm and leg as high as possible**
➡ **Perform movement with control**

10 SIDE BRIDGE

Abunassar: "This is pure oblique work, mostly for endurance. If you don't shrug your shoulder and keep it stable, then you will really feel a burn in the side closer to the ground."

- Lie on side with elbow underneath

- Raise body onto elbow and feet

- Lower to start position; repeat for specified reps

- Perform on opposite side for specified reps

COACHING POINTS

➡ **Keep body in straight line from shoulder to feet**
➡ **Pull shoulders back** ➡ **Keep core tight**
➡ **Thrust upper hip toward ceiling**

STANDING DUMBBELL PRESS

Abunassar: "Standing forces you to contract your core to stabilize the weight overhead."

- Begin in hip-width stance with dumbbells at shoulder level

- Without arching back, drive dumbbells up until arms are straight and dumbbells overhead

- Lower to starting position; repeat for specified reps

COACHING POINTS

- ▶ **Keep back straight and head up**
- ▶ **Avoid using body for momentum**
- ▶ **Go through full range of motion**

CHAUNCEY BILLUPS' TRAINING GUIDE

STRENGTH TRAINING — LEVEL 3

Days 1, 3

Upper Body Lifts	Sets/Reps
Dumbbell Chest Press	3 X 10
Seated Rows	3 X 10
Push-ups	3 X 15
Reverse Grip Pulldown	3 X 10
Seated Shoulder Press	3 X 10

Lower Body Lifts	Sets/Reps
Single-Leg Dumbbell Squat	3 X 10
Single-Leg Romanian Deadlift	3 X 10
Walking Dumbbell Lunge	3 X 10

Core	Sets/Reps
Physioball Weighted Sit-up	3 X 10
Single-Leg V-up	3 X 10
Alternate Arm/Leg Supermans	3 X 10
Side Bridge	3 X 10

Day 2

Upper Body Lifts	Sets/Reps
Standing Single-Arm Cable Chest Press	3 X 10
Standing Single-Arm Cable Row	3 X 10
Single-Arm Lat Pulldown	3 X 10
Standing Dumbbell Press	3 X 10

Lower Body Lifts	Sets/Reps
Single-Leg Leg Press	3 X 10
Hamstring Physioball Roll-up	3 X 10
Physioball Bridge Holds with Weight	3 X 45 second hold

Core	Sets/Reps
Physioball Weighted Sit-up	3 X 10
Single-Leg V-up	3 X 10
Alternate Arm/Leg Supermans	3 X 10
Side Bridge	3 X 10

STRENGTH TRAINING — LEVEL 2 Days 1, 2, 3			STRENGTH TRAINING — LEVEL 1 Days 1, 2	
Upper Body Lifts	**Sets/Reps**		**Upper Body Lifts**	**Sets/Reps**
Standing Single-Arm Cable Chest Press	3 X 8		Standing Single-Arm Cable Chest Press	3 X 8
Plyometric Push-ups	3 X 10		Plyometric Push-ups	3 X 10
Standing Single-Arm Cable Row	3 X 8		Standing Single-Arm Cable Row	3 X 8
Reverse Grip Pulldown	3 X 8		Reverse Grip Pulldown	3 X 8
Medicine Ball Woodchop Throw	3 X 10		Medicine Ball Woodchop Throw	3 X 10
Standing Dumbbell Press	3 X 8		Standing Dumbbell Press	3 X 8

Lower Body Lifts	**Sets/Reps**
Dumbbell Step-ups	3 X 8
Power Step-ups	3 X 8

ON-COURT TRAINING

DRILL	REPS	SETS	TIME	EL
Flexibility/Active Warm-up				
Ball handling			5 min	1
Dribble series—perform from right wing, top, left wing			60 min	
1 dribble right	Make 7 each spot	1		3
1 dribble left	Make 7 each spot	1		3
FTs	Make 2	1		
Jab right · 1 dribble left	Make 7 each spot	1		3
Jab left · 1 dribble right	Make 7 each spot	1		3
FTs, get water	Make 4	1		
Jab right · 2 dribbles left	Make 7 each spot	1		3
Jab left · 2 dribbles right	Make 7 each spot	1		3
FTs	Make 3	1		
Jab right · 1 dribble left, step back, move left	Make 7 each spot	1		3
Jab left · 1 dribble left, step back, move right	Make 7 each spot	1		3
FTs, get water	Make 4	1		
1 dribble right, crossover dribble	Make 7 each spot	1		3
1 dribble left, crossover dribble	Make 7 each spot	1		3
FTs	Make 3	1		
1 dribble step back, crossover, get to basket	Make 7 each spot	1		3
FTs, get water	Make 4	1		
Backpedal, 1- and 2-dribble pull-ups	Make 10 each wing	1		3
Spot shooting [5 spots]	Make 10 each spot	1	10 min	2

CHAPTER 2

DWIGHT HOWARD

EDITOR'S NOTE

Although an explanation about why Dwight Howard is this book's cover athlete is probably unnecessary, we'll go ahead and lay it out anyway. Howard personifies the goals of basically every training-conscious man out there, whether a professional athlete, weekend warrior, or beach body. The NBA superstar possesses massive, rock-solid chest, shoulder, and ab muscles, and the guy can jump out of the gym, rip down rebounds, and run the court like the shiftiest of point guards. Howard is the perfect blend of athlete and muscle man.

Our interview and training shoot with Howard took place during the 2007-08 NBA season, when the young big man was becoming a bigger and bigger blip on America's radar. He had been an All-Star the previous season, but Howard didn't truly make his mark until he won the 2008 Slam Dunk Contest wearing a Superman cape. Since literally soaring into household-name status, Howard has established himself as one of the best centers in the league and is on schedule to accomplish his goal of being the best ever at the position.

DWIGHT HOWARD'S PLAY CONTINUES TO SOAR THANKS TO WORKOUTS IN WHICH THE LONG, LEAN SUPERSTAR TACKLES MUCH MORE WEIGHT THAN ONE MIGHT EXPECT.

Regular training sessions with Magic S+C coach Joe Rogowski have contributed mightily to Howard's ascension. The two get together for strength training with weights much heavier than you'd ever expect a long-limbed basketball player to lift. We were actually surprised at what took place in the Magic's weight room that day, as Howard casually benched 365 pounds, then repped out on lat pulldowns with the entire weight stack.

Since then, we've never been surprised by Howard's consistent on-court improvement and accomplishments. The Magic is now the team to beat in the East, and Howard's production is the team's main driver. His combined averages for the past two seasons are 20.7 ppg and 14 boards per contest. This double-double average and his NBA Defensive Player of the Year Award in 2009 are testament to his all-around athletic ability.

This is the Dwight Howard cover feature as it first appeared in the January/February 2008 issue of *STACK* Magazine.

SUPER FREAK

Dwight Howard was once skinny and doubted.

As a seventh-grade point guard for Southwest Atlanta Christian Academy, Howard was often overshadowed by players at larger schools in the hotbed of A-Town prep basketball. "I was really skinny and went to a smaller Christian school. No one thought I'd ever make it out or do anything with my basketball career," he recalls. "I kept my trust and faith in God. He told me that if I kept him first in my life, He'd take care of the rest."

Not much changed for Howard in his eighth-grade season. Despite his claims, nobody believed that the 5'10" skinny kid could throw it down. That is, until he gathered his friends on the basketball court and said, "Watch this!" Howard drove toward the hoop, elevated, and dunked the ball in front of everyone, offering a glimpse of the kind of ability that was growing inside him. Still, by his own account, "It was like a Reggie Miller dunk. I didn't move the rim or the backboard, and the net didn't even shake. I was still happy about it, though."

Dwight Howard grew up fast.

Once Howard entered high school, he began growing into the freakish form we know today. He made varsity immediately and was moved to power forward, due in large part to the fact that he sprouted seven inches in one year to hit 6'9". Throughout this growth spurt and position change, Howard maintained the footwork, quickness, elevation, and ball control he had as a guard, making him unstoppable against small-school opponents.

As a junior, Howard led SACA to the Class A State Championship game and finally achieved

the recognition his extraordinary ability warranted. "In 11th grade, I started to get NBA scouts coming to my games and workouts," Howard recalls. "That felt great, but I tried to stay away from all that so my teammates didn't think I was above them."

Howard may have acted the same, but his game certainly changed. As a senior, he led his team to the state title, averaging 26 points, 18 boards, 8 blocks, and 3.5 assists per game. His final high school campaign earned him the Naismith, Morgan Wootten, Gatorade, and McDonald's National Player of the Year awards. For this clean sweep of the awards season, Howard was named Mr. Basketball in the State of Georgia.

The Magic's choosing him straight out of SACA as the first overall pick in the 2004 draft was the first of many memorable moments for Howard. Others include All-Star Games and near 30-30 nights. Howard is now posting stats that are increasingly ridiculous, and he's on his way to becoming one of the best to ever play the center/power forward position.

An impressive demonstration of Howard's athleticism was seen during the 2007 Slam Dunk contest. The sight of a big man throwing down dunks with the dexterity of a little man, the hang time of Michael Jordan, and superhuman thunder caught even the most critical dunk enthusiasts off guard. "I was so excited to be in my first dunk contest last year," Howard says. "I don't know why, but I got out there in front of all the people, and it was real. I got nervous at first, but then I got it done."

Dwight Howard is 6'11", 265 pounds.
Watching a 265-pound tower of explosive muscle dance across a weight room in coordinated movements is unsettling. Everything you've assumed about the human body is suddenly questioned. Your mind struggles to register what's in front of you, and you think to yourself: He can't be that big. He shouldn't be able to move like that.

But he is, and he can.

The skinny kid from Atlanta is no more, and for Howard, only the memory remains. But that memory fuels the big man's desire. "I remember when I used to be really skinny," he says. "And because of that, I've always wanted to have nice arms with big triceps and big biceps. I want to continue to make my chest real big and get my abs nice. This helps me as a basketball player, too; because when I'm like this and in tip-top shape, it helps me avoid injuries. I plan on spending a lot of time in the weight room lifting, so I can play for a very long time."

Howard's inspired time in the weight room has translated into the bigger, stronger body he covets. Although not the best indicator of athletic improvement, Howard uses the bench press to gauge his progress with weights. Among his more memorable moments was his recent successful attempt at benching 365 at home. "That felt really good," he says, "because I remember in high school my dad [taking] me to the gym and I couldn't bench press one plate."

Enter Joe Rogowski.
Because Howard doesn't perform all of his training at home, a lot of credit has to go to Orlando strength coach Joe Rogowski, who joined the Magic two years ago. Since then, Rogowski has laid out a training regimen that's constantly helping Howard thicken up and gain power. "Joe has done an excellent job of staying on me about lifting," Howard says. "I told him I want to be a great player, and we decided that lifting weights is something [to] help me achieve that in the long run. Since he got here, he's provided me with a schedule that makes

sure my body is always on point. A lot of people tell me that I don't realize how strong I am, but I know that I haven't come close to my peak strength yet."

Rogowski never met the skinny Dwight Howard, but he's more than impressed with the latest version. "Howard is unique in that he's got that genetic ability to do pretty much anything we put in front of him," he says. "He's naturally strong and naturally gifted in every sense. He's just a freak when it comes to strength, power, and speed. You couldn't ask for a better physical specimen."

Howard gives Rogowski plenty to work with, but his freakishness does pose one problem—a good one. "It's tough to set goals for a guy like this, because there aren't any other athletes who are where he is," Rogowski says. "He has already broken every physical goal imaginable for an NBA player. And as he gets older, he gets more powerful naturally. So we do our best to keep him strong and on the court through injury prevention."

What next?

How will the dynamic big man, whose favorite on-court activity is blocking shots, amaze us next? Howard has a pretty good idea of what we will see: "I want to be one of the greatest players to ever play this game. I want our team to be a championship team. In the future, I know that our team can be, and will be, a championship team."

The opportunity to become one of the best big men in NBA history sits before Howard. Based on how he handles other opportunities, things could get ugly for the rest of the league. Just listen as Howard explains how he takes advantage of an open lane: "When I see an opening to the rim, I think whether anybody else is going to jump first, and that makes me want to jump even higher. I just want to dunk it as hard as I can and rip down the whole goal."

Dwight Howard was once skinny and doubted.

Dwight Howard's Strength Training

Dwight craves heavy weight, so once a week he and Rogowski head to the Magic weight room to perform the following heavy lifts. "This training is a pure strength and power workout," Rogowski says. "Sometimes Dwight likes to meathead out and lift a lot of weight and get strong. I let him know that lifting these heavy weights is good for his strength and psyche, but we need to counterbalance it with some stability, balance, or proprioception exercises, which we do once or twice a week."

Use Dwight's three preferred lifts to feed the meathead within.

STRENGTH TRAINING

BENCH PRESS

Rogowski: "The bench press is about total upper-body power and strength. Dwight uses this pyramid rep scheme to build endurance, strength, and, most importantly for his position, the power of his fast-twitch muscle fibers. In basketball, we're not trying to overdo it with weight, especially in-season. That's why we don't do maxes with one rep. The last set of two reps is generally a weight Dwight can handle comfortably while still stressing his muscles."

- Lie with back on bench, gripping bar slightly wider than shoulder width

- Keeping lower back on bench and elbows tight to sides, slowly lower bar until it touches chest

- Drive bar up until arms are straight

- Repeat for specified reps

COACHING POINTS

➡ Keep core activated ➡ Don't arch back
➡ Avoid using body for momentum ➡ Go through full range of motion

LAT PULLDOWN

Rogowski: "This is one of the main rebounding exercises Dwight does. When you're getting close to 20 boards a game, you have to be strong with your upper body, pulling down. This also counterbalances any chest exercises we do that day. We always like a 1-to-1 relationship with chest-to-back work. We really work on good posture and balanced strength with our guys so we can avoid any shoulder injuries."

- Sit on lat pulldown machine and grip bar overhead, slightly wider than shoulder width

- Without rocking back, pull bar down in front until it touches upper chest

- Allow bar to rise back to start position until arms are straight

- Repeat for specified reps

COACHING POINTS

- ➡ Keep back as straight as possible
- ➡ Avoid using body for momentum
- ➡ Go through full range of motion
- ➡ Keep head up throughout exercise

LEG PRESS

Rogowski: "We like to do multi-joint exercises when possible, and this is a great one for the lower body. It gets all the muscles around your hips, knees, and ankles stronger. We generally go heavier on this, because it is a safer exercise. You're not putting the back at risk, like other exercises do, such as the squat, [which makes] taller players' backs go into hyperextension. For someone like Dwight, who already has back hyperextension, we try to stay away from that. We keep the reps low since we go heavy on this."

• Assume position on leg press machine with feet slightly wider than hips

• Lower weight sled with control until knees are bent 90 degrees

• Drive weight up by extending legs to start position

• Repeat for specified reps

COACHING POINTS

➡ **Perform with control** ➡ **Go through full range of motion**
➡ **Maintain slight bend in knees**

DWIGHT HOWARD'S TRAINING GUIDE

STRENGTH TRAINING

EXERCISE	SETS/REPS
Bench Press	1 X 10; 1 X 8; 1 X 6; 1 X 4; 1 X 2
Lat Pulldown	2-4 X 10-12
Leg Press	3-4 X 6-8

CHAPTER 3

STEVE
NASH

EDITOR'S NOTE

In the world of professional sports, picking a performance training role model can be a little tricky. A guy might be incredibly fast, chiseled, or explosive, but his training methods could be garbage. His physical attributes might have developed in spite of his training, not *because of* it. For our last cover feature of 2008, we ignored such naturally gifted physique freaks and set our sights on a two-time NBA MVP who earned every single bucket, assist, and steal with hard work and thorough preparation.

Although Steve Nash has been the league's top player twice, he looks more like a svelte skateboarder than an NBA superstar. For just that reason, Nash was overlooked and doubted during his high school days in Canada, his college career at Santa Clara, and even after his first few NBA seasons. In the face of doubt and distrust, Nash kept his focus and snuck up on everyone who said he was too slow, too small, or just too damn physically unimpressive. For all that, we loved him as a *STACK* cover athlete.

STEVE NASH DIRECTS THE PHOENIX SUNS' OFFENSE DURING A GAME AGAINST SAN ANTONIO. NASH'S WORKOUTS HELP HIM SURVIVE THE GRUELING NBA SEASON.

Another upside of a Steve Nash cover feature was the opportunity to sit down again with Erik Phillips, the Phoenix Suns' expert strength and conditioning coach. Observing Phillips and Nash interact was like watching a Zen master train his most serious student. Respecting Phillips and appreciating his wealth of knowledge, Nash dove headfirst into studying the methods behind Phillips' training.

After witnessing Nash's preseason workout, we watched him put his training to use during the 2008–09 NBA season, when he threw in 15.7 ppg and dished out 9.7 dimes per game—numbers that fell slightly short of his MVP runs, but were pretty impressive for a guy who turned 35 halfway through the season.

This is the Steve Nash cover feature as it originally appeared in the November/December 2008 issue of *STACK* Magazine.

THE PERFECTIONIST

As the steely-eyed general of the Phoenix Suns, Steve Nash rules the court without the slightest hint of caution in his game. Whether fighting through a pick, absorbing an errant elbow to the ribs, or hitting the floor after one of his commanding drives, Nash shows little regard for his body. Off the court, it's a completely different story.

Steve Nash's incredible awareness of every detail of his body has propelled him to two NBA MVPs and 13 successful professional seasons. Since the start of his basketball career back in Canada, the 6'3" guard has been constantly honing, perfecting, and developing all aspects of his athleticism. As a result, he's drawn every ounce of performance and ability out of his wiry body to reach the pinnacle of the basketball world.

By now it should be passé to doubt Nash, or even to bring up the fact that he doesn't look the part of an NBA star. That was kind of a fad in the mid-'90s, when every major college coach in the U.S. had Nash's videotapes showing up on his desk. The footage showed an undersized point guard at St. Michael's University School crossing over fellow Canucks, mercilessly dominating entire defenses. Yet coaches rejected Nash's scholarship applications, doubting his ability to take on quality competition. "People have always doubted me," Nash says, recalling that experience. "I used to keep all of the rejection letters I got back in a shoebox. I held onto that for a while as motivation. I was given one scholarship offer, to Santa Clara University."

Despite its underwhelming size, Santa Clara proved to be a big opportunity for the imported point guard. Nash flourished under head coach Dick Davey, and the team made national noise during his four years there. The Broncos plowed

into the NCAA Tournament as a No. 15 seed, shocking high-powered Arizona one year and taking out Maryland in another. It was during his career at Santa Clara that Nash got used to being underestimated and running with [and putting down] bigger, higher-rated opponents.

Nash's collegiate career, combined with his impressive performance at the Nike Desert Classic, garnered enough attention before the 1996 NBA Draft to convince the Suns to take him as the 15th overall pick. Many times, this is when an athlete can stand up, call out his doubters and say, "Look at me now!" Not for Nash, though.

"Fortunately, I was somehow a first-round draft pick," he says. "But I was still doubted that I'd have a long career in the NBA. Then I was doubted that I would be a starter, and doubted that I'd be an All-Star. At every level that I've taken it, I've always had naysayers."

Now sitting atop the game, Nash has proven the doubters wrong with every milestone and award earned throughout his NBA career. He no longer keeps rejection letters stuffed in a shoebox, but Nash doesn't have to look far for motivation. "I would say the last few years there have been a lot of people supporting me," he says. "I seem to have overcome [being doubted] only to find that now I'm an 'old man' and I'm 'over the hill' [laughs]. That's good though; that's what I'm used to. I wake up every morning as an underdog, regardless of the awards or the amount of years of success I've had."

The perpetual underdog started 81 games for the Suns in 2007–08, supplying his team with more than 11 assists per game and shooting 90 percent from the foul line and about 43 percent from behind the arc. Nash continues to elevate his game by refusing to overlook any part of his

preparation—in season or out. "I set goals for myself and know I work hard throughout the season and throughout the off-season so that I have peace of mind," he says. "If things don't go well, I know that I've worked as hard as I can. It puts me in a good state when I'm slumping and not playing well. I don't feel like I'm second-guessing the amount of work I've put in. It eliminates a whole psychological barrier that I would have to overcome if I felt like I had been cheating myself."

Nash's exhaustive approach demands an incredible amount of time and dedication, along with help from one of the league's best, Suns' strength coach Erik Phillips. Phillips acknowledges that Nash is an immaculate pupil. "His work ethic is always perfect," Phillips says. "He maintains a level of strength and stabilization throughout the whole year, so we will take little steps here and there preseason, during the season, and postseason. Steve's an unbelievable athlete who is so in tune to his body. He knows what he needs to work on and what he needs to lay off of. Anything I ask him to do, he is the poster child for the correct technique."

Nash's ability to talk the strength and conditioning talk proves that Phillips isn't exaggerating the point guard's knowledge: "Erik's philosophy of [using] corrective exercises, which help you correct deficiencies as an athlete and prevent injuries down the road, is a great baseline to set any training regimen by," Nash says. "His ability to use functional training to get gains off the court, which allows you to transfer more easily onto the court, is another way to become more athletic and better prepared for the longevity of the season and the competition at this level."

Every off-season, Nash and Phillips work to get Nash's body strong enough to support the reckless style and hustle that define his game. "Most of the strength component of Nash's workout is [centered around making him able to] absorb blows on the court—fighting through picks, getting knocked down, getting fouled," Phillips says. "We're working on Steve being the first off the ball and beating a person to a spot."

Nash adds, "My training goals are always to get into great shape so that I can prevent injury and that I'm well prepared to take on the competitive level and pounding it takes to get through a season. We're trying to find ways to get a little more athletic, stronger, more powerful, quicker, and with better endurance. We're always trying to get little gains every day, at the same time having the thoughtfulness to go about it the right way to prevent injury."

This goal is achieved through adherence to the philosophy of the National Academy of Sports Medicine: build the base of the pyramid first, then build the top. In Nash's case, stability is the base, with the rest comprising strength, then power. Not surprisingly, Nash grasped this concept when we met up with him. "Today we [did] a chest and back workout," he says. "We were looking for strength and power gains, while at the same time adding elements of instability so we can work the total body. We use an unstable plane—whether it be on the [physio]ball or one leg—to create a more challenging and athletic approach to isolating a muscle group."

The workout Nash performed consists of three chest exercises and three back exercises, all of which incorporate the entire body. Perform the following exercises one after another; rest for a few minutes, then perform a second set of each.

EXERCISES

PHYSIOBALL SINGLE-ARM DUMBBELL BENCH

Phillips: "Your glutes are working to maintain stabilization. Steve's gaining chest strength through the dumbbell press, and he's also using his core muscles to stay in that position and not fall off the ball."

- Lie with upper back on physioball, holding dumbbell at chest

- Assume bridge position with shoulders, hips, and knees in straight line and heels directly under knees

- Drive dumbbell toward ceiling until arm is straight

- Lower with control; repeat for specified reps, then switch pressing arm

COACHING POINTS

- ➡ Don't lean to side during press
- ➡ Use nice, even motion
- ➡ Don't allow hips to sag

2

ALTERNATING SINGLE-ARM MED BALL PUSH-UP

Phillips: "Alternating your hands on the med ball makes you use your shoulder stabilizers and puts your pecs in a different range of motion on each side. You're also doing a functional movement, because outside of playing offensive line, you're never pushing straight ahead with two hands at the same time. Steve is always going one way or another, [and] we're trying to mimic that."

- Assume push-up position with one hand on med ball

- Perform push-up until both arms are straight

- Roll med ball to other hand; perform push-up

- Continue in alternating fashion for specified reps

COACHING POINTS

➡ Keep body in plank position with core and glutes tight

3 SPLIT-STANCE MED BALL CHEST PASS

Phillips: "This incorporates a little more power, but he's using all of his stabilizers to stay in a split stance. You're catching [the ball] in the same spot and throwing it as hard as you can against the wall. The chest pass is a basic basketball movement, so Steve can use the same follow-through movement he would on a chest pass. This also helps him [to] be able to catch a pass from a teammate."

- Stand about six feet from wall in split stance holding med ball at chest

- Explosively fire med ball into wall, obtaining full extension with arms and hands

- Catch ball at chest; immediately throw it again

- Repeat in continuous fashion for specified reps

COACHING POINTS

➡ Lock out back leg by firing glute ➡ Slightly bend front knee

4 PHYSIOBALL SINGLE-ARM DUMBBELL ROW

Phillips: "This is the same basis as the chest press except it's a back exercise, which helps prevent the shoulders from rotating forward from chest work. This allows for gains on both sides of the body and prevents you from over-demonstrating one plane of your body. The single-arm aspect makes him stabilize in the opposite direction of the weight so that he doesn't fall off the ball."

- Lie with chest on physioball, holding dumbbell with arm extended toward floor

- Pull dumbbell to chest by driving elbow toward ceiling

- Lower dumbbell with control; repeat for specified reps

COACHING POINTS

➡ Stabilize on ball and use core and glutes to lock body into place
➡ Avoid jerking up or hitting physioball with dumbbell
➡ Use fluid motion around ball

5 SINGLE-LEG, SINGLE-ARM ROW

Phillips: "Try to get the non-balancing leg up to 90 degrees; it really gets your glute and core stabilizers working on the balancing leg. Making that glute work will help maintain your hip posture. Your instincts are going to make you want to twist, but if you twist on a single leg, you'll fall down. This is just like going up for a lay-up; you're in a single-leg position with your knee driven up to 90 degrees, and you're required to make an upper-body movement based on where your defender is going. Also, when you're coming down from a rebound, you come down on one leg and need to stabilize on that glute."

- Assume single-leg stance with slight bend in knee

- Hold cable attachment on same side as standing leg with arm extended forward

- Raise opposite knee to hip level, bending leg to 90 degrees

- Pull handle to chest by driving elbow back

- Return handle to start position with control; repeat for specified reps

COACHING POINTS

➡ Don't twist or jerk body during movement
➡ Don't allow balancing knee to rotate internally or externally

6 OVERHEAD MED BALL THROW

Phillips: "Steve is doing a back exercise with this soccer-type throw over his head. He's using his back muscles both to throw the ball and catch the ball coming back overhead. This is similar to any time Steve has to make an outlet pass or get into a weird motion. For example, he might be on a single leg, falling backwards, and has to wait for the defender to go by to make a quick pass. Or when he fakes a shot, and he's got the ball above his head in the first place, but decides to make a different angled pass from overhead. We are adding the weight of the med ball as a strength component."

- Stand about six feet from wall in split stance, holding med ball overhead

- Explosively fire med ball at wall with overhead motion

- Catch ball overhead; immediately throw it again

- Repeat in continuous fashion for specified reps

COACHING POINTS

➡ Lock out back leg by firing glute
➡ Slightly bend front knee

STEVE NASH'S TRAINING GUIDE

	SETS/REPS
Physioball Single-Arm Dumbbell Bench	1 X 10; 1 X 12
Alternating Single-Arm Med Ball Push-Up	1 X 10; 1 X 12
Split-Stance Med Ball Chest Pass	1 X 10; 1 X 12
Physioball Single-Arm Dumbbell Row	1 X 10; 1 X 12
Single-Leg, Single-Arm Row	1 X 10; 1 X 12
Overhead Med Ball Throw	1 X 10; 1 X 12

CHAPTER 4

ALLEN IVERSON

EDITOR'S NOTE

Allen Iverson is known for his athletic, game-changing style of play, not for the quality of his off-court preparation. In fact, AI's legendary "we talkin' about practice?" rant pretty much sums up how people perceive his work ethic as an NBA player. But shortly after AI moved from Philadelphia to Denver, we got a call from Nuggets strength coach Steve Hess—and we had a serious decision to make.

A respected industry leader, Hess told us that Iverson had rededicated himself and was actually working hard in the weight room to put on five pounds of quality muscle. Hess assured us that he could "teach an old dog new tricks!" Intrigued and curious, we decided to head out to Denver in the fall of 2007 to see exactly what Iverson had gotten himself into.

As we watched, Hess put Iverson through a quick and intense strength training routine that sought to accentuate the slashing point guard's already-impressive athletic attributes. After working steadily for about 30 minutes, Iverson told us that throughout his 10-plus years in the NBA, he had never spent time training off the court, but that Hess had inspired him to put in a solid effort

ALLEN IVERSON'S AGGRESSIVE STYLE OF PLAY LEADS TO MANY FREE-THROW ATTEMPTS, BUT IT ALSO REQUIRES THAT HE PREPARE HIS BODY FOR THE PHYSICAL POUNDING IT TAKES.

after each practice. We have to be honest: Allen Iverson pumping iron in the Nuggets' weight room was a strange sight. But there was nothing strange about the results.

Iverson claimed that he felt stronger and more explosive on the court, and his subsequent numbers confirmed that to be true. During the second half of the 2006-07 season, he had averaged 24.8 ppg with 7.2 assists. The following season, he started all 82 games for the Nuggets, averaged 26.4 points, and helped lead Denver to the NBA Playoffs.

Although Iverson's career arguably entered the twilight phase when he joined the Detroit Pistons, the training he did with Hess undoubtedly elevated his game for an additional few years.

This is the Allen Iverson cover feature as it first appeared in the November/December 2007 issue of *STACK* Magazine.

NO MERCY

Guarding Allen Iverson just got scarier. The man with the most explosive crossover in the NBA is muscling up this year, devoting himself to a new weightlifting routine. By focusing on strength, Iverson is adding yet another superior athletic attribute to his already filthy game, bringing it to an almost unfair level. Showing no sign of pity for the rest of the league, Iverson is positioning himself for the kill—in the form of an NBA Championship.

Although it's early in the NBA season, you can see a noticeable difference in Allen Iverson as he walks across the Denver Nuggets' weight room. Is it his slightly thicker shoulders? Maybe. But it could be his newly chiseled arms, too. Truth be told, the big change is the fact that Iverson is here—in the weight room—working with team strength coach Steve Hess.

Once criticized in Philly for the way he conducted himself during mandatory practices, Iverson now knocks out voluntary weightlifting sessions after practice. So why has the 12-year NBA icon decided to stick around and work out after practice? Straight from The Answer himself: "To just get strong. That's my motivation."

Iverson is a true athlete, and Hess backs it up. "My man AI is one of the world's greatest athletes," he says. For more than a decade of NBA stardom, Iverson built his name and 27.9 points-per-game career scoring average on incredible talent, confidence, heart, and toughness. Much of his talent is God-given, and early athletic success grew his confidence. His last two defining qualities, though, are byproducts of time spent on the streets and football fields of his hometown of Hampton, Virginia.

In high school, AI was the state's best quarterback, and he played just as impressively at defensive back. Football's contact and violence drew Iverson to the gridiron and kept basketball a distant second. But as his hoops game developed, Georgetown took notice and offered him the opportunity to play. So Iverson hung up his cleats and brought his love for contact to the hardwood. As it turned out, his heart and toughness ended up defining him as a player—the game's hardest driving point guard. Iverson showed no regard for the consequences to his body. And that's exactly why he and Hess have set out to reshape and strengthen it.

After thousands of points scored, many unsuccessful playoff runs, and a weak supporting cast in Philly, Iverson has found new opportunity in Denver. "It's been really cool since I got here," AI says. "It's been like a fresh start for me."

Although he's started new things, Iverson has maintained others—notably his on-court productivity. After joining the Nuggets last season, he averaged almost 25 points and more than seven assists a game. Throw in two steals per contest, and Iverson shapes up as one of the most prolific point guards in the history of the game.

His impressive numbers and the Nuggets' resulting success [they made it to the Western Conference finals last year] have left him gleaming. In fact, he lights up when he talks about his new home and strength coach, something that never would've happened back in Philly. "I have a lot more excitement with this training and working with Steve," he says. "I never had a real interest in lifting before, but Steve's assured me that this is going to help me be a better player and add some years to my career. He knows what he's doing. From the moment I got here, a lot of the guys were telling me that it would be good for me to work with him."

Yes, Iverson is approaching the later years of his career. But look for this season to be his best to date. Just ask the guy who's responsible for getting him ready. "That stuff about not being able to teach an old dog new tricks? That's garbage," Hess says. "Just watch what happens with my guy. Watch AI with his new muscle as he makes the All-Star team again, and we win the NBA Championship."

AI's Muscle Formula

Hess is expecting serious results from Iverson's new dedication to his weightlifting routine. "AI has made a commitment to become

© AP Images

a beast," he says. "We're going to put on five pounds of quality muscle during the season. Right now, he's 170 pounds and five percent body fat. We're going to increase his strength and get him up to 175 pounds."

Given the grueling nature of Iverson's game—and the long NBA season—balance is a crucial element in Iverson's routine. "The guy is truly unbelievable. He plays so hard every night," Hess says. "He's going to play 44 minutes a night, which adds up. He's been in the league for 12 years; his [training] program reflects that. It's very important that we don't overload him so that we don't take anything away from his hoops. We want him to progress slowly and stay healthy, so [we reach our] primary goal—making sure that everything is functioning correctly."

Iverson appreciates and thrives on this health-oriented, gentler approach. "Steve's not coming in here and trying to kill me every day," Iverson says. "He's just trying to [give] me the right amount of work to help me as a player. It's a whole new experience, because I come in here after practice—after being a little burnt out—

and he'll give me a few things to get me better and get me out of here. I don't care too much about getting really big, but Steve [will] help me get strong and be able to take a lot more punishment."

Hess has Iverson move quickly through the entire workout to keep the intensity and efficiency high. "We superset everything with AI," Hess says. "He doesn't have a lot of time, so I want to make sure everything is firing when he's in here. We alternate between upper- and lower-body lifts so we can work his entire body each session, three to four times per week."

AI's rep scheme of 1x9, 1x13, and 1x16 appears simple at first glance, but Hess has a fairly complex and scientific reason for it. "A lot of times when you use a 10-rep scheme, routine takes the place of thought," Hess says. "By creating an unusual rep scheme, you are exercising your mind and body. It is imperative to remember that you still need to construct your reps according to the specific body response you want."

Try Iverson's new weightlifting routine, in circuit fashion, after practice.

EXERCISES

CROSSOVER SYMMETRY POSTERIOR DELT

Hess: "It's important that you do this quickly and stay stable with a good 'C' position in your back. This strengthens the posterior delts, but we do it in a standing stabilizing position so we can work on Al's defense as well."

- Assume athletic stance, with lower back in "C" position, facing crossover symmetry band hook-up

- Hold handles in front with straight arms so bands cross over each other

- Keeping arms straight, quickly bring them back and to high position [overhead in "V"]; return to start position

- Repeat to middle position [shoulder-level] and low position [pointing down in "V"]

- Repeat sequence for specified reps

Variation: If crossover symmetry equipment is not available, attach small bands to squat rack

Benefits: Posterior delt and core stabilizer strength // Defensive ability

Hess: "This works single- and double-arm movement, just like the game of basketball does. I make sure my man AI is getting full extension on every rep."

• Sit on iso chest press machine

• Perform six chest presses with both arms

• Perform remainder of reps by alternating one arm at a time

Variation: If iso chest press is not available, perform on incline bench with dumbbells

Benefits: Single-arm, double-arm, and upper-body strength

3

LATERAL MED BALL STEP-UP WITH RESISTANCE

Hess: "A basketball player's first three steps are among the most important things, [especially for] a point guard. This exercise not only works on getting AI's quads, hamstrings, and glutes to fire in the correct sequence, it also simulates his holding a basketball, while it works on his stability and balance."

- Assume athletic stance with plyo box to right

- Hold med ball in front and have partner provide bungee resistance from left

- Push off left leg, open right hip toward box and place right foot on top of box

- Explode up onto box using right leg, while simultaneously raising med ball overhead and driving left knee toward chest

- Step down to start position; repeat for specified reps

- Perform set on other side

Benefits: Improved explosion, balance, and stability

EXERCISE	
	SETS/REPS
Crossover Symmetry Posterior Delt	1 X 9, 1 X 13, 1 X 16
Alternating Iso Chest Press	1 X 9, 1 X 13, 1 X 16
Lateral Med Ball Step-Up with Resistance	1 X 9, 1 X 13, 1 X 16

CHAPTER 5

AMAR'E STOUDEMIRE

EDITOR'S NOTE

We spent the day with Amar'e Stoudemire in the midst of his excruciatingly long rehabilitation from microfracture knee surgery. At that time, it was a crapshoot whether an athlete would ever truly recover from that procedure. We knew Stoudemire was one of the most athletic and best overall big men in the NBA, but running a cover feature about a guy who wouldn't be playing for quite awhile, if ever again, didn't necessarily fit our mold.

Until we met Stoudemire, our content had focused on training experts and methods that helped the world's top athletes improve their on-field performance. And although Stoudemire was training with Phoenix Suns strength and conditioning coach Erik Phillips, one of the best in the business, we had to wonder if the info would be valuable to our readers, because Stoudemire was in no position to perform.

Our time at the Suns' training facility was unlike any previous shoot. We were granted access to intimate details of Stoudemire's past experiences and current struggles, as he opened up to us about his childhood, family life, and aspirations—all pieces that shape Stoudemire's existence. At

AMAR'E STOUDEMIRE RECOVERED HIS AMAZING POWER GAME THANKS TO AGGRESSIVE REHABBING AFTER MICROFRACTURE KNEE SURGERY.

that time, our magazine didn't include such content about an athlete, but we had a considerable amount of non-training information that was too powerful to keep from our readers.

So for the first time, our cover feature told a story—one of a young, gifted basketball player who broke free from poverty and worked his way to the top of the game. We also wrote about how Stoudemire complemented his commitment to the Suns' training room and gym with mental strength, as his return to the hardwood was an everyday, every minute thing. Our readers needed to know what was required for such an epic return.

Although the personal content separated this cover feature from previous ones, the training information Phillips provided was second-to-none. He blended functional strength, stability, and flexibility into a beautiful routine that sought to make Stoudemire a more athletic player once he regained full health.

This is the Amar'e Stoudemire cover feature as it first appeared in the March 2006 issue of *STACK* Magazine.

EXPECT ME

Lake Wales, Florida, is a trap. It's a place where guns, drugs, and crime prevail over jobs, college degrees, and opportunity, a place where children watch family members try to obtain a life outside of the city's suffocating grip only to fail. Considering all that can confine a man within this city's boundaries, the rare escape is even more impressive.

God blessed the child that can hold his own. These powerful words—inked across Amar'e Stoudemire's chest—sum up his experience in Lake Wales. When he was 12, he lost his father to a heart attack. Shortly thereafter, he saw his mother sent to jail. But as this child was forced to become a man, his strength grew inside and out. His blessings of physical power, mental courage, and overall fortitude helped him get through life's most painful situations.

Being virtually parentless in a small, dark town wasn't Stoudemire's only struggle. The local preacher, to whom Stoudemire's mother entrusted him, was arrested. Shady AAU coaches and other hangers-on constantly looked to benefit from his basketball potential. In search of the perfect fit and a stable household, Stoudemire transferred through six high schools, only to be deemed ineligible for his junior season by transfer rules.

After shaking the rust off from his inactive junior year, Stoudemire used his senior season at Cypress Creek High School to prove his worth to NBA scouts. And after eight GMs balked at the 6'10", 250-pound man-child with a troubled past, the Phoenix Suns took him as the ninth overall selection in the 2002 draft, officially signaling his escape from The Trap.

Stoudemire's rookie season was nothing short of historic; he became the first ever straight-from-high school pick to win NBA Rookie of the Year. He used the next two seasons to polish his raw and powerful game. In 2004–05, Stoudemire achieved All-Star status and tallied 26 points per game. He topped off his season averaging 37 points in the Western Conference Finals against Tim Duncan and the San Antonio Spurs. Things were looking good for Stoudemire, who was positioned as the favorite for 2005–06 League MVP. In the words of Shaq himself after he faced Stoudemire and the Suns, "I've seen the future of the NBA, and his name is Amar'e Stoudemire."

The future was put on hold though, as Stoudemire faced yet another struggle. The knee soreness he experienced in the off-season severely increased during preseason. Doctors determined that Stoudemire needed microfracture surgery to repair damaged cartilage in his knee. The process consists of drilling several small holes in the bone around the knee joint, causing bone marrow and blood to seep out, form a clot, and release cartilage-building cells. The clot will eventually become firm repair tissue to replace the damaged cartilage. Recovering from microfracture surgery is an extensive four- to six-month process, which many professional athletes fail to conquer. However, Stoudemire's youth and determination, combined with the fact that his knee suffered no additional damage, created a positive outlook for his return.

The child who held his own is back at it as a man trying to reconquer a sport. "When I got hurt, I knew I had to remain positive," Stoudemire says. "I became even more determined and went into attack mode. I know I'm going to come back stronger than ever, and,

as a team, we will accomplish our ultimate goal. Just wait and see."

Across the Suns' workout board, Stoudemire has scribbled some borrowed words from his inspiration, Tupac Shakur. Take it as a message—or a warning—but nevertheless, take it: "Expect me like you expect Jesus to come back. I'm coming."

Program Goals

Helping Stoudemire ready his body for its return to dominance is Phoenix Suns head strength and conditioning coach Erik Phillips.

Stoudemire on Phillips: "Erik and his program have helped me in the past, and will have me ready to come back. I got stronger and

© AP Images

more explosive out on the court when I first started working with him."

Although Stoudemire credits Phillips for his strength increases, he deserves some props himself. Phillips says that Stoudemire was in tremendous shape heading into this season because of the hard work he did in the off-season. "After losing the Western Conference Finals, he was so hungry that he was willing to do anything to achieve his ultimate goal, and that's why this injury is such a shame. You'll see how hard he has been working once he gets back."

The training Stoudemire used in high school is completely different from that which Phillips employs. "I started working out my junior year with the typical high school mentality of trying to bench as much as possible," Stoudemire says. "Now I realize the important things I have to do to make me better on the court, like the flexibility and balance work I do with Erik."

Unfortunately, the mentality Stoudemire refers to is common among ballers, according to Phillips. "I see a lot of guys who like to sit down on the leg extension machine and just pump away. That is ineffective for improving performance, and it creates strength imbalances. Even guys who have done the important stuff correctly, like core work, might have strength, but don't know how to use it."

Therein lies the beauty of Phillips' program. It develops proper muscle balance, corrects kinetic chain imbalances [how muscles work in conjunction with one another], and establishes optimum multidirectional body control through a combination of corrective exercises, flexibility work, stabilization, and functional strength training. The result? A body that works better. In discussing goals he specifically set for Stoudemire, Phillips says,

"When we first started, I was nervous about doing anything that would get in the way of his natural gifts. He is a freak of nature. I've never seen a player this powerful before."

Phillips supplements Stoudemire's God-given ability with upper body and core strength work. This helps him handle the banging from opposing centers, who are often bigger, and maintain his rep as a quick, explosive offensive threat.

Corrective Exercise Training

With the help of the National Academy of Sports Medicine [NASM], Phillips evaluates each player three times a year—preseason, midseason, and postseason—using the NASM Body Map. The test consists of two movements—a squat with arms overhead and a single-leg squat with hands on hips—while photos are taken from various angles. Phillips examines the images to determine weaknesses in posture, movement, strength, flexibility, and overall athleticism, and then creates a personalized program to correct them.

"Although corrective work doesn't take much time to complete—only about 15 minutes—it's probably one of the most beneficial things we do around here," Phillips says. "One of our main goals is to keep these guys healthy and feeling good throughout the 82-game regular season, playoffs, and off-season workouts. This corrective work has allowed us to be successful with that."

The corrective exercises rectify muscle imbalances, recondition injuries, prepare the body for training, prevent training overload, enhance adaptation, and improve the body's work capacity and stabilization strength. If these terms sound foreign to you, think about it this way: these exercises help you get the most out of your body by making it more receptive to training and by making it work more efficiently.

AMAR'E'S BODY MAP
Squat with Arms Overhead

OBSERVATION	DEFICIENCY
Feet turn out	Weak abductors, tight adductors
Knees move outward	Weak abductors, tight adductors
Excessive forward lean	Tight hip flexors, weak glutes/erectors

Single-Leg Squat with Hands on Hips

OBSERVATION	DEFICIENCY
Knee moves inward [R, L]	Tight adductors
Leans over grounded leg [R, L]	Lack of hip stabilization

Foam Roller Calf Complex
- Sit on ground with foam roller placed between right calf and floor
- Slowly roll it up and down muscle; repeat with other leg

Phillips designed the following corrective work specifically for Stoudemire. However, because these deficiencies are common among basketball players, the routine can benefit all. Complete the exercises before every game, practice, or training as a warm-up.

Foam Roller

For all foam roller exercises, roll slowly over specified region for 30-60 seconds until you identify a tender area. Hold roller on tender spot for an additional 30 seconds before continuing. This will loosen soft tissue and decrease soreness within your muscles.

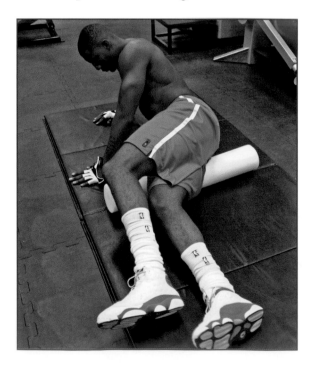

Foam Roller TFL-IT Band

- Lie on right side supporting body with right arm
- Place foam roller between floor and outside of right thigh
- Move left leg to front of body and place that foot flat on ground
- Starting at hip, slowly roll between hip and knee; repeat for opposite side

Adductor Complex

- Lie on your stomach using your elbows as support
- Situate right leg out to side; place foam roller under and perpendicular to inside of right thigh
- Slowly roll from groin to inside of knee without letting lower back hyperextend
- Repeat with other leg

Static Stretching Exercises

Bring each stretch to slight point of tension, and hold for 30 seconds. Make sure to perform every stretch on both sides.

These improve functional flexibility of hips, hamstrings, glutes, and calves.

Slant Board Calf Stretch

- Begin with left foot in front of right on slant board; keep right leg straight
- Lean forward, keeping right heel flat, until you feel tension in that calf; don't allow foot to collapse inward

Piriformis Stretch

- Lie on back
- Bend right leg and cross it over left leg, which should remain straight
- Place left hand on outside of right knee and slowly pull right leg toward left shoulder until you feel slight tension in glute

Kneeling Flexor Stretch

- Kneel on right knee and bend left leg 90 degrees with foot flat on ground
- Tighten glute of right leg and rotate pelvis under while maintaining upright posture

Progression 1:
While maintaining pelvic position, raise right arm up and over to elongate the spine

Progression 2:
Slowly rotate torso backward

Standing Hamstring Stretch

- Place right foot on an elevated surface in front of you; angle it toward left leg, and tilt pelvis forward
- Maintain pelvic position while slowly leaning forward until you feel slight tension in your right hamstring
- Repeat with left leg

Strengthening Exercises

Perform 2 sets of 15 reps for each exercise. Make sure to train both legs on directional and single-leg exercises.

These exercises eliminate muscle imbalances by strengthening glutes, core, abductors, and adductors.

Lateral Tube Walking

- With elastic tubing around both ankles, stand with toes straight ahead, knees over feet and hands on hips
- Draw abdomen in and step right while maintaining upright posture; don't rock your upper body when stepping
- Step again with left foot, bringing your feet back to shoulder-width distance; repeat for 15 steps

Standing Hip Abduction

- Wrap elastic tubing around lower right leg and stationary object
- Stand with left leg closer to stationary object
- Move right leg outward; pause for two seconds
- Return leg to starting position

Standing Hip Adduction

- Wrap elastic tubing around lower right leg and stationary object
- Stand with right leg closer to object
- Move right leg forward and over left leg; pause for two seconds
- Return leg to starting position

Stability Ball Squat

- Place stability ball between mid-back and wall
- With control, squat keeping your knees aligned over your second and third toes
- To return, activate glutes and stand upright until hips and knees are straight

Stability Ball Bridge with Abduction

- Place elastic tubing around both knees, and lie with upper back on stability ball
- While keeping your feet flat and knees pointed straight ahead at shoulder-width, rise into bridge position
- Apply pressure into tubing, draw in abdomen, activate glutes, and lift pelvis up as far as possible without arching low back
- Hold bridge for two seconds; slowly lower to start position

Single-Leg Balance Reach

- Assume single-leg stance
- While keeping balancing leg slightly bent and hip in line with knee, draw in abs and tighten glutes
- With opposite leg straight, extend it backward 45 degrees, tightening glute, quad, and calf
- Stabilize for two seconds and bring foot back toward opposite foot

Rebuilding Amar'e

What does an NBA superstar do in the weight room 10 weeks out from serious knee surgery? Everything he can.

After completing daily corrective exercises and rehabilitation work with head athletic trainer Aaron Nelson and assistant Mike Elliott, Stoudemire enters the Suns' weight room, removes his oversized T-shirt, pops his man Tupac into the CD player and prepares for the workout Phillips has for him that day.

Phillips modifies some of Stoudemire's off-season workouts to create post-rehab lifts that focus on upper-body strength—avoiding stress on the newly repaired knee. However, Phillips includes exercises where Stoudemire stands and balances on one leg. He says, "Single-leg exercises are great rehabilitation work for his knee. All of the muscles around the joint strengthen because they have to stabilize his body weight throughout the set."

A few sets into the workout, Stoudemire takes a break from mouthing the lyrics booming overhead and grins as he looks down at his suddenly swollen physique. He says, "I tend to get big really fast. I have to be careful not to lift too much weight or I'll blow up. My brother is about my height. He lifts a lot and is 320 pounds—all muscle."

Agreeing, Phillips says, "Because he can't do a lot of running, we were a little worried about him getting too big and heavy. He weighed 253 last year, and he's been able to stay between 255 and 258 since his injury. We have done a pretty good job of keeping him light so he'll stay quick and explosive when he gets back on the court."

Consequently, Stoudemire's workouts are geared toward developing functional strength in conjunction with stabilization strength, instead of building size. Stoudemire accomplishes this by fatiguing a muscle group with a strength exercise, and then performing a stabilizing exercise with the same muscle group. He completes each exercise once, and then repeats the routine.

Check out what "The Future" has been doing to get court-ready, and of course, why he's doing it.

EXERCISES

1 PUSH-UP WITH ROTATION

Phillips: "This motion requires a tremendous amount of shoulder stabilization. When you get to the top of the rotation, the bottom shoulder is supporting and balancing a great deal of body weight, and your core has to work to keep your body rigid and in line."

- Perform push-up

- At top of movement, rotate body into side-plank position with one arm on ground and other extended toward ceiling

- Slowly rotate back to top of push-up position

- Perform push-up; repeat rotation to opposite side

Benefits: Strengthens chest // Shoulder and core stability

COACHING POINTS

➤ Do not allow hips to dip when you rotate into side position

➤ Make whole body rigid—especially your core—so body forms one straight line

➤ Ankles, knees, hips, lumbar spine, and shoulders should all be on same plane

2 PUSH-UP ON BOSU BALL

Phillips: "I have Amar'e replace the Push-Up with Rotation with the Bosu the second time through. The Bosu's unstable surface forces his whole upper body—core included—to work to maintain balance."

- Assume push-up position with hands holding outside of upside-down Bosu ball

- Perform push-up

Benefits: Strengthens chest // Works core strength and shoulder stability

COACHING POINTS

➤ Keep core tight to remain stable and body in straight line

3 SEATED ROW

- Sit at row machine with chest against pad and butt back

- Keeping elbows tight to sides, pull handles back until hands are close to chest

- Slowly return to start position; repeat for specified reps

COACHING POINTS

- ➡ Don't use momentum to pull handles
- ➡ Perform with control

4 SINGLE-ARM, SINGLE-LEG CABLE ROW

Phillips: "When Amar'e is on one foot with the other leg elevated, his glutes, hips, core, and all the muscles around his ankle work hard to provide a stable base."

- Assume single-leg stance with opposite leg bent 90 degrees so thigh is at hip level

- Hold handle with hand on the same side as balancing leg

- Pull cable until hand is at chest level

- Return cable to starting position with control

Benefits: Develops balance and stability while working back muscles

COACHING POINTS

- ➡ Don't rock back as you pull the cable ➡ Keep core tight and body balanced on each rep
- ➡ Make sure balancing leg lines up directly under corresponding hip and shoulder
- ➡ Don't allow upper body to lean toward side of balancing leg to compensate for the instability

5 SEATED DUMBBELL CURL TO SHOULDER PRESS

Phillips: "This exercise incorporates two movements into one, which allow you to train multiple muscles in less time. The curl portion works the biceps, the transition works the rotator cuffs, and the overhead press works the deltoids and traps."

• Sit on bench holding dumbbells at sides

• Perform dumbbell curl until weights are shoulder level

• Rotate palms so they face away; perform overhead shoulder press

• Lower dumbbells through same motion with control

COACHING POINTS

➥ Keep core tight

➥ Don't arch back during overhead press

STABILITY BALL SHOULDER COMBO

• Lie with chest on stability ball and light dumbbells in hands

• Keeping arms straight, raise dumbbells to front, side, and rear for one complete repetition

Benefits: Works entire range of motion of shoulder joints // Strengthens front, side, and rear delts, and upper back muscles, including rhomboids // Stability ball works core stabilization

COACHING POINTS

➥ Move dumbbells with control; don't swing them with momentum created by stability ball

➥ Flex glutes and abs to provide stable base so you don't move all over the place

7 TRICEP EXTENSION WITH CURL BAR

- Lie with back on bench holding curl bar over chest with straight arms

- Without changing position of upper arms, lower bar to top of forehead

- Raise bar back to start position

Benefits: Strengthens triceps

COACHING POINTS

➡ Do not allow elbows to get wider than shoulder width when lowering or raising bar

➡ Keep feet flat on floor and knees hip width

8 SINGLE-LEG TRICEP PUSHDOWN WITH BASKETBALL GRIP

Phillips: "The muscles around your ankle and knee of the balancing leg have to work to maintain balance throughout the exercise. The basketball grip gets our guys used to gripping the ball—making it more basketball-specific."

- Assume single-leg stance in front of cable pushdown with opposite foot just off ground

- Keeping elbows tight to ribcage, push cable down until arms are straight

- Allow arms to return to start position with control

Benefits: Strengthens triceps // Works balance and stability

COACHING POINTS

➡ Keep elbows pinned to your sides for whole set; upper arms should not move

➡ Make sure balancing leg is directly under corresponding hip and shoulder

➡ Don't lean upper body to side of balancing leg to compensate for instability

9 STABILITY BALL CRUNCH WITH MED BALL TOSS

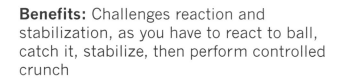

- Sit on stability ball facing partner who's holding med ball

- As he tosses ball to you, catch it and perform crunch

- At top of crunch, throw ball to partner with chest pass

Benefits: Challenges reaction and stabilization, as you have to react to ball, catch it, stabilize, then perform controlled crunch

COACHING POINTS

➡ Keep core tight to absorb force of throw and to prevent stability ball from moving

10 STABILITY CRUNCH AND TWIST WITH MED BALL

- Sit on stability ball facing partner who's holding med ball

- As partner tosses med ball to you, catch it, twist to right, twist to left, and then perform crunch

- At top of crunch, throw ball back to partner with chest pass

Benefits: Works reaction, stabilization, and rotational core strength

COACHING POINTS

➡ When twisting right, twist until you can touch your right elbow to stability ball and vice versa twisting left

STABILITY BALL BRIDGE WITH ADDUCTION

• Place upper back on stability ball with med ball between your knees

• Rise into bridge position by flexing glutes; create straight line from knees to shoulders

• Lower with control

Benefits: Strengthens glutes and upper hamstrings, which, according to Phillips, are the body's most powerful muscles used in jumping and explosive movements // Squeezing ball between knees works adductors

COACHING POINTS

➤ Focus on flexing glutes and applying force to med ball between knees
➤ Keep stomach drawn in and knees and toes hip-width apart and pointing straight ahead

DUMBBELL BENCH PRESS

• Lie with back on bench, holding dumbbells near front of shoulders

• Drive dumbbells to ceiling until arms are fully extended

• Lower dumbbells to start position; repeat for specified reps

COACHING POINTS

➤ Bring dumbbells together at the top of the movement
➤ Bring dumbbells down as deep as possible with control
➤ Keep core tight
➤ Inhale on way down; exhale on way up

AMAR'E STOUDEMIRE'S TRAINING GUIDE

AMAR'E'S POST-REHAB LIFT

EXERCISE	SETS	REPS	REST IN SECONDS
Dumbbell Bench Press	2	12	0-60
a. Push-Up with Rotation	2	12	0-60
b. Push-Up on Bosu Ball	1	12	0-60
Seated Row	2	12	0-60
Single-Arm, Single-Leg Cable Row	2	12	0-60
Seated Dumbbell Curl to Shoulder Press	2	12	0-60
Stability Ball Shoulder Combo	2	8	0-60
Tricep Extension with Curl Bar	2	12	0-60
Single-Leg Tricep Pushdown with Basketball Grip	2	12	0-60
Stability Ball Crunch with Med Ball Toss	2	12	0-60
Stability Ball Crunch and Twist with Med Ball	2	12	0-60
Stability Ball Bridge with Adduction	2	12	0-60

Integrated Stabilization Training (IST) improves neuromuscular efficiency, functional strength, core strength, dynamic stabilization, and functional flexibility.

WEEK 1 — PHASE: IST

STRENGTH	EXERCISE	SETS	REPS	INTENSITY	REST	NOTES
Total Body	Dumbbell Front Step-up and Bicep Curl to Press	2	20	60%	0 sec	20 total presses—10 on each leg
Chest	Stagger Stance Double-Arm Cable Chest Press	2	20	60%	0 sec	10 presses w/ each leg forward
Back	Double-Arm, Single-Leg Cable Row	2	20	60%	0 sec	20 total rows—10 on each leg
Shoulders	Single-Leg Shoulder Scaption	2	20	60%	0 sec	20 total—10 on each leg
Legs	Stability Ball Squat	2	20	60%	90 sec	Hold DBs for extra resistance

WEEK 2 — PHASE: IST

STRENGTH	EXERCISE	SETS	REPS	INTENSITY	REST	NOTES
Total Body	Dumbbell Side Step-up and Bicep Curl to Press	2	15	65%	0 sec	15 total presses—7/8 on each leg
Chest	Dumbbell Bench: Alternate Arm	2	15	65%	0 sec	15 presses each arm
Back	Single-Arm, Single-Leg Cable Row	2	15	65%	0 sec	
Shoulders	Single-Leg Cable Tricep Pushdown	2	15	65%	0 sec	15 total push-downs—7/8 on each leg
Legs	Single-Leg RDL	2	15	65%	90 sec	Hold DB in op-posite hand for extra resistance

WEEK 3 — PHASE: IST

STRENGTH	EXERCISE	SETS	REPS	INTENSITY	REST	NOTES
Total Body	Dumbbell Multi-Planar Step-up and Bicep Curl to Press	3	15	65%	0 sec	15 total presses—7/8 on each leg
Chest	Stability Ball Dumbbell Chest Press	3	15	65%	0 sec	
Back	Stability Ball Dumbbell Row	3	15	65%	0 sec	1. Front 2. Side 3. Rear
Shoulders	Stability Ball Shoulder Combo	3	15	65%	0 sec	
Legs	Single-Leg Squat Touchdown	3	15	65%	90 sec	Hold DB in op-posite hand for extra resistance

WEEK 4 — PHASE: IST

STRENGTH	EXERCISE	SETS	REPS	INTENSITY	REST	NOTES
Total Body	Chest Squat to Row	3	12	70%	0 sec	
Chest	Stability Ball Single-Arm Dumbbell Chest Press	3	12	70%	0 sec	12 presses each arm
Back	Stability Ball Single-Arm Dumbbell Row	3	12	70%	0 sec	12 rows each arm
Shoulders	Single Leg Lateral Raise	3	12	70%	0 sec	12 total raises— 6 on each leg
Legs	Single-Leg Squat	3	12	70%	90 sec	

Stabilization Equivalent Training (SET) increases muscle mass and enhances metabolism, stabilization strength, and endurance during functional movement patterns.

WEEK 5 — PHASE: SET

STRENGTH	EXERCISE	SETS	REPS	INTENSITY	REST	NOTES
Chest	a. Dumbbell Chest Press b. Push-up with Rotation	2	12 12	70%	0 sec	
Back	a. Seated Row b. Single-Arm, Single-Leg Cable Row	2	12 12	70%	0 sec	
Shoulders	a. Seated Dumbbell Shoulder Press b. Single-Leg Lateral Raise	2	12 12	70%	0 sec	
Legs	a. Front Dumbbell Lunge b. Side Step-up to Balance	2	12 12	70%	120 sec	

WEEK 6 — PHASE: SET

STRENGTH	EXERCISE	SETS	REPS	INTENSITY	REST	NOTES
Total Body	Dumbbell Lunge, Curl/Press	3	10	75%	0 sec	
Chest	a. Dumbbell Incline b. Stability Ball Dumbbell Chest Press	3	10 10	75%	0 sec	
Back	a. Pulldown b. Single-Arm, Single-Leg Cable Row	3	10 10	75%	0 sec	
Legs	a. Leg Press b. Front Step-up to Balance	3	10 10	75%	0 sec	

WEEK 7 — PHASE: SET

STRENGTH	EXERCISE	SETS	REPS	INTENSITY	REST	NOTES
Total Body	Dumbbell Squat, Shrug, Calf Raise	3	8	80%	0 sec	
Chest	a. Bench Press b. Stagger Stance Cable Chest Press	3	8 8	80%	0 sec	8 total presses—4 w/ each leg forward
Back	a. Pull-up b. Single-Leg Shoulder Extension	3	8 8	80%	0 sec	
Legs	a. Dumbbell Side Lunge b. Single-Leg RDL	3	8 8	80%	120 sec	

WEEK 8 — PHASE: SET

STRENGTH	EXERCISE	SETS	REPS	INTENSITY	REST	NOTES
Chest	a. Dumbbell Bench Press b. Stagger Stance Single-Arm Cable Chest Press	4	8 8	80%	0 sec	
Back	a. Seated Row b. Single-Arm, Single-Leg Cable Row	4	8 8	80%	0 sec	
Shoulders	a. Standing Lateral Raise b. Single-Arm Single-Leg Shoulder Press	4	8 8	80%	0 sec	
Legs	a. Dumbbell Walking Lunge b. Single-Leg Squat Touch-down	4	8 8	80%	120 sec	

CHAPTER 6

BRANDON
ROY

EDITOR'S NOTE

Brandon Roy's first NBA season was undoubtedly bittersweet. Although the young guard from the University of Washington tallied impressive stats and won the 2006–07 NBA Rookie of the Year Award, the Portland Trail Blazers were otherwise dismal, winning only 32 games all year.

Knowing that Roy was way too athletic and talented to be overshadowed by anything, we headed to Portland to find out what sort of training had been fueling the rising star. During the workout we observed, Roy did not disappoint, validating our decision to feature him in *STACK* Magazine. At one point, the high-flying guard decided to show off for the cameras and a small group of friends by jumping onto a 40-inch box—while holding a dumbbell in each hand. During a quick break, he sank a back-to-the-basket half-court shot with unsettling nonchalance. In addition to these impressive feats, Roy also performed various quickness and explosion exercises as part of an intense session with his trainer, Travelle Gaines.

During our interview, Roy mentioned that at the Blazers' preseason camp, his teammates had immediately noticed the positive effects of his off-season training. And once the 2007–08 season

BRANDON ROY RISES ABOVE A PAIR OF TIMBERWOLVES PLAYERS FOR A SHOT. ROY'S TRAINING REGIMEN HAS HELPED HIM IMPROVE HIS GAME EACH YEAR.

began, he put his elevated game to good use by leading Portland to a more-than-respectable 41-41 record. The following season, Roy took another big step [with the Blazers still on his back], averaging 22.6 points and 5.1 assists per game and leading the Blazers to 54 wins, tied with Denver and San Antonio for the second-best record in the West.

This is the Brandon Roy training feature as it originally appeared in the April 2008 issue of *STACK* Magazine.

SLUMP KILLER

I don't believe in that superstitious stuff. I believe in hard work and preparation. I'm going to go out there and prove that to people who might have predicted [a sophomore slump]. – Brandon Roy

Portland Trail Blazers shooting guard Brandon Roy has lived his entire life by one motto: Stay hungry and humble. "I've applied those two things to everything I've done," he says, "and they continue to keep me moving forward in life."

Winning the 2007 NBA Rookie of the Year Award hasn't weakened Roy's hunger at all, because he knows its implications. "If you look at the players who have won that award, it speaks for itself," says the 6'6" former Washington Husky. "Now that I'm in the same class as guys like Tim Duncan and Michael Jordan, I have to do my best to win a championship."

Despite winning the award and his rookie line of nearly 17 points, four boards, and four dishes per game, NBA pundits and fans were still predicting a "sophomore slump," ascribing Roy's stats to beginner's luck.

So far this year, though, Roy has backed up his All-Star status by tallying nearly 20 points per contest. Undisputedly, he's one of the best guards in the NBA.

And while he loves dealing helpers that get the crowd on its feet, Roy knows what makes him most dangerous: "My biggest weapon," he says, "is my size. I can handle the ball and break my guy down off the dribble, [and] I can still shoot pretty well."

Hungry as ever, Roy spent the months leading up to this season attacking two main goals: becoming more explosive and getting lean. "I looked back at how I played my rookie season and saw some weaknesses in my game," he says. "I wanted to increase my explosiveness and maybe lose a little weight so I could be stronger throughout 82 games."

To accomplish these tasks, Roy joined up with SPARQ Master Trainer Travelle Gaines. After a full summer of jumping, twisting, and squatting through different Gaines-inspired exercises and drills, Roy entered the Blazers' training camp ready to test his progress. "Within two to three weeks, my teammates were telling me that I looked a lot leaner, faster, and much quicker," Roy says. "It was obvious right away."

Gaines noticed the results, too. "Physically, he looks much more mature," he says. "He's more ripped and well-defined. He says he feels a lot faster, and he appears to be much quicker. As a basketball player, he needs that great explosiveness, change of direction, acceleration and, more important, first-step quickness."

Gaines attributes Roy's amped physical performance to his internal qualities. "He challenged me every single time we worked out," Gaines recalls. "He always wanted more,

so it was always a challenge for me to see how far I could take him—and a challenge for him to see how far he would let me take him. He is a total professional; his whole life revolves around being a better basketball player."

With a willing client, Gaines could apply his philosophy to the fullest. "I like to cater to what the athlete needs to accomplish," he says. "There can be no cookie-cutter approach to this."

Catering to Roy's desire to be more explosive and leaner, Gaines developed a workout that combines plyometric, explosive, core, and flexibility training in a routine that is guaranteed to stop a predicted slump in its tracks.

© AP Images

EXERCISES

LATERAL SHUFFLE WITH RESISTANCE BANDS

- At baseline, assume defensive stance with resistance bands around ankles

- Perform defensive shuffle to midcourt and back

Benefits: Mimics playing defense in basketball game // Strengthens hip flexors // Improves lateral movement

COACHING POINTS

- ➤ Sit butt back, keep chest up with feet facing straight forward
- ➤ Do not click heels together
- ➤ Begin first set at half speed; second set increases to three-quarter speed, then remaining sets at full speed

DUMBBELL SQUAT PRESS

- Stand with feet shoulder-width apart, holding dumbbells on top of shoulders

- Sit back, then lower into squat

- Explode up out of squat onto balls of feet while pressing dumbbells overhead

- Repeat for specified reps

Benefits: Works lower body // Mimics explosive movements you make on basketball court— going up for a jump shot or to grab a rebound

COACHING POINTS

- ▶ Keep weight on heels, with chest up and shoulders back
- ▶ Explode out of squat using legs to press weight
- ▶ Lower with control

- Stand with resistance bands around ankles, holding med ball

- Step forward with left foot and lower into lunge position

- Hold position, then rotate upper body to left, with ball

- Bring right foot forward, so it's even with left foot

- Perform to right side

- Repeat in continuous fashion for specified distance

Benefits: Works hip flexibility and oblique muscles, because you have to squeeze your core while rotating // Bands add extra resistance for more hip and overall leg strength; the more hip flexibility and mobility you have, the more explosive you can be

COACHING POINTS

- Bring foot over opposite calf every time you step into lunge
- Keep chest up and shoulders back
- Do not over stride lunge
- Follow the med ball with your eyes during each rotation

DUMBBELL CLEAN PULL TO ARMPIT

• Assume clean position with dumbbells out to sides at shin level

• Explode through hips, knees, and ankles while shrugging with straight arms

• Drive elbows toward ceiling to bring dumbbells to armpits

Benefits: Builds explosiveness, because it is a total body, triple-extension exercise

COACHING POINTS

➡ Keep chest up, shoulders back and weight on heels in starting position
➡ Lower dumbbells slowly for an eccentric effect
➡ Explode up using legs to lift weight

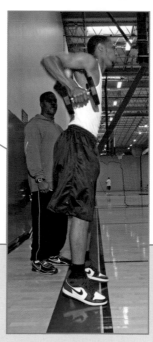

DUMMBELL BOX JUMPS

Gaines: "When we work with athletes of Brandon Roy's caliber, a 42-inch plyo box just isn't enough for them. So we started to add weight. Brandon got to a point where he could jump onto a 36-inch box holding 60-pound dumbbells. He starts with no weight and then works up—15, 25, 40, then 55 or 60."

- Assume athletic position about an arm's length away from plyo box

- Lower into quarter-squat, then explode through hips, knees, and ankles to jump for maximum height

- Land softly with bent knees on top of plyo box

- Step down slowly; repeat for specified reps

- Add weight as your skill advances

Benefits: Builds explosive power to help you jump for rebounds, block shots, dunk, and even lay a ball up

COACHING POINTS

➡ Perform first set with no weight, then gradually increase weight with each set

➡ Focus on keeping proper squat form and exploding up

6 OVERHEAD MED BALL TOSS

- Assume sit-up position with partner in front of you

- Catch med ball from partner overhead and perform sit-up

- Throw ball back to partner on way up

- Repeat for specified reps

Benefits: Develops total core strength // Works transverse abdominal muscles

COACHING POINTS

- ➡ Use 15- to 20-pound med ball
- ➡ Throw ball back to partner halfway through sit-up

7 SIDE MED BALL TOSS

- With partner to left, sit on ground with knees bent and heels just off ground

- Receive ball from partner, rotate right, touch med ball to ground, then throw ball back

- Repeat for specified reps; perform set on other side

Benefits: Strengthens the core, mostly your obliques

COACHING POINTS

- ➡ Sit back until abs are engaged to support body
- ➡ Follow med ball with eyes ➡ Keep feet inch off ground
- ➡ Use 15- to 20-pound med ball

SPLIT-SQUAT JUMPS WITH RESISTANCE BANDS

- Assume split-squat position with resistance bands around ankles

- Lower slightly, then jump straight up for maximum height

- Switch position of legs in air, landing in split-squat position with opposite foot forward

- Continue for specified reps

Benefits: Works explosiveness from different positions

Coaching Points

- Feet should be walking-step-distance apart in split-squat position
- Keep knee behind toes, chest up and shoulders back

EXERCISE	Sets	Reps
Lateral Shuffle with Resistance Bands	4	15
Dumbbell Squat Press	3	10
Resistance Band Walking Lunge with Med Ball Rotation	4	10
Dumbbell Clean Pull to Armpit	4	6
Dumbbell Box Jumps	5	5
Overhead Med Ball Toss	2	50
Side Med Ball Toss	2	25 each side
Split-Squat Jumps with Resistance Bands	3	10

CHAPTER 7

CHRIS PAUL

EDITOR'S NOTE

When we overheard Chris Paul address a New Orleans Hornets team rep as "Sir," we almost lost it. One of the more refreshing moments in our professional sports experience, that interaction confirmed our belief that Paul—in addition to being one of the NBA's best point guards—is a humble, hard working, and dedicated team leader; and it set the tone for our entire time with him.

We met up with Paul during the fall of 2007, when he returned to the hardwood after earning NBA Rookie of the Year honors the previous season. The Hornets were living out of suitcases and practicing at a tiny college in Oklahoma City following Hurricane Katrina. Despite dealing with natural-disaster-induced chaos on a daily basis, and despite incredible soreness and fatigue from a game and travel the night before, Chris Paul was completely cool.

Hornets strength coach Jack Manson worked closely with the slashing guard to improve his strength, durability, and capacity for recovery. To keep Paul on the court and playing at a high level, Manson prescribed various balance exercises, which strengthen his ankles, as well as foam rolling and flexibility drills to keep him limber and ache-free. All of this was tested a few weeks later when

CHRIS PAUL ABSORBS THE CONTACT AND GOES UP FOR A SHOT AGAINST THE SPURS. PAUL'S WORKOUTS FOCUS ON INJURY PREVENTION, AMONG OTHER PHYSICAL NECESSITIES.

Paul landed awkwardly on an opponent's foot and badly sprained his ankle. Injuries like that cannot be prevented, but the resulting damage can be limited. And Paul's prep with Manson did exactly that, allowing him to get back on the court much sooner than expected.

At the time of our visit with Paul, he was known by many as the NBA's next big thing. Since then, he has lived up to that billing by becoming a two-time NBA All-Star and turning the lowly Hornets into perennial playoff contenders.

This is the Chris Paul cover feature as it originally appeared in the February 2007 issue of *STACK* Magazine.

DRIVING FORCE

As Chris Paul enters the Southern Nazarene University weight room on this particular morning, all the Hornets present—vets and rookies alike—perk up. A voice from the back of the room yells,

"There's the man of the hour!"

No hint of sarcasm or razzing can be detected in these words; they simply announce that the team's leader has arrived.

The New Orleans/Oklahoma City Hornets have been shuffling into their temporary home in Bethany, Oklahoma, since 9:30 a.m. Amidst SNU athletes and power-walking senior citizens, the players take their places to begin the morning's training session and practice. The team arrived from New Orleans in the middle of the night after a turbulent flight, and their star point guard's usual confident strut is noticeably subdued. All the mad dashes to the hoop he made last night have left him severely sore and fatigued.

But you wouldn't know any of this by the look on Paul's face. A huge, warm smile spans from ear to ear. The reigning NBA Rookie of the Year has a lot of reasons to be smiling today. A good bet would be on the career-high 16 assists he dished out against division rival Houston Rockets. Other solid guesses would be that he's the hero of two cities, the most-liked player in the NBA, and one of the brightest young stars in the league.

During Paul's rookie campaign, he averaged 16.1 points and 7.8 assists a night, led the NBA in steals with 175, and spearheaded the Hornets' 20-game improvement over the previous season's win total—numbers that demonstrated his superior ability as a point guard. However, the most powerful effect Paul had on his team cannot be quantified. At the age of 21, Chris Paul naturally assumed the role as the team's leader, making everyone around him a significantly better player. "He drives this whole team," says Scott

Cochran, assistant strength and conditioning coach for the Hornets. "Older guys—who have been in the league a lot longer—watch what he does each day, then go out and try to emulate him. They might try to do the same thing, but it's usually not as good. Chris isn't afraid to grab you and let you know you're doing something wrong. He's our true leader."

Paul's leadership by example is innate, and he's comfortable demonstrating it. "I've always been a natural leader," he says. "I am all about accountability, so for me to be the point guard and leader of this team, I need to make sure [the team] sees me working hard and doing the right things. It's all about me being accountable and setting that example."

Blessed with basketball skills since the day he started playing the game, Paul first received recognition at West Forsythe High School in Lewisville, North Carolina. As his team's high-profile star baller, he soon realized how greatly his decisions and actions impacted the people around him. Paul wholeheartedly accepted his status as a role model and lived his life accordingly, especially after high school.

Besides earning ACC Rookie of the Year honors and distinguishing himself as the third overall selection in the NBA Draft after two seasons at Wake Forest, Paul stood out as a polite, selfless, and humble student-athlete. "I am totally comfortable being looked at as a role model," he says. "It feels good to give kids someone to look up to. They retain everything and do what they see other people doing, so I know it's important to set the right example."

Asked about the source of his strong values, Paul answers without pause: "It's all a testament to my family and how my parents raised my brother and me. My entire family has always been my biggest influence and inspiration; they are always there with me."

Paul's relationship and experiences with his grandfather, Nathaniel Jones—"Papa Chilly" to those who knew him—may be most responsible for shaping Paul into the person he is today. The owner and founder of Jones Chevron, the first African-American-owned service station in North Carolina, Papa Chilly was known, respected, and loved by everyone in the area. Paul spent much of his childhood by his grandfather's side, helping him change oil filters and clean windshields. Their bond grew stronger as Paul grew older. When he signed his letter of intent to play for Wake Forest, a proud Papa Chilly was the one who placed the Demon Deacons hat on Paul's head after the ceremony.

The day after Paul signed with Wake, his excitement and happiness ended suddenly and tragically, when he learned that a group of thugs had robbed and murdered Papa Chilly—news that crushed Paul and his family. Confused and angry, Paul needed a way to deal with these unfamiliar emotions. His aunt suggested doing something that would help Paul cope with the loss, while simultaneously honoring his grandfather. She suggested that in his next game Paul should go out and try to score 61 points—one for each year of his grandfather's life. Paul obliged, attempting to do what seemed impossible at the time. By halftime, Paul had racked up 32 points, and he was up to 59 with three minutes remaining in the contest. Paul received the ball, drove the lane, laid the ball in, and got fouled. With his emotions rising to the surface, Paul stood at the foul line and purposely airballed his free throw, preserving his 61-point tribute. Exiting the game, he went to the sidelines and fell into his father's arms.

"My late grandfather will always be with me," Paul says. "He worked hard every day and had to deal with some difficult situations, but he never gave up. When he was facing something tough on the job, he always fought through it. That is what I took from him—I never give up. When there is an obstacle in front of me, I fight right through it."

The will and drive that Papa Chilly instilled in Paul are the force behind his basketball prowess. Having led the Hornets into the NBA's upper echelon, Paul is motivated to fight through to an even higher level. "As a team, we are going to build on last year," he says. "We won 38 games, but that wasn't enough. Anything less than the playoffs this year will be a disappointment to us. Personally, I'm looking for an all-around improvement by increasing my percentages in every category—free throws, threes, and field goals. I really want to improve my assist-to-turnover ratio, too."

Although Paul missed most of last month with an unpreventable ankle sprain, he will be back soon, elevating his game in each of these categories. The rest of the Hornets will take notice and follow their leader.

High Gear

Every time Paul goes to the hole, he drives just as hard as he did when scoring Papa Chilly's 60th and 61st points back in high school. A relentless, powerful, and slashing style defines Paul's game—so much so that he's often referred to as a one-man fast break. The Hornets' head strength and conditioning coach, Jack Manson, and Cochran are the two men who keep Paul's high-speed game in gear.

"I love watching him when he gets the ball and decides to push it," says Cochran, whose background is in big-time football. "When he hits that drive, he looks like Barry Sanders or Emmitt Smith hitting a hole. He has that type of power and quickness, but he's always in control."

Looking at Paul—who's an even 6 feet and 175 pounds—you might doubt his ability to man up with the bigger players around the league. Manson and Cochran concede that Paul is smaller than most NBA point guards, but they quickly assert that he's a seriously strong dude. "When someone goes against CP for the first time, it's always the same response," Manson says. "They say something like 'Damn, CP is so strong.' It's tough to hang with him on the court."

Cochran affirms Paul's unexpected strength. "Even when he first got here," he says, "Chris was way ahead when it came to training, because he is naturally so strong. When we were benching the other day, he repped out 225 six times like it was nothing."

Paul's near-mastery over speed, strength, and power posed an interesting challenge for the men whose job is to make players faster and stronger. "He had such a great base when he got here that we actually had to look for his weaknesses," Cochran says. "We focus on all the small things with him."

Manson has put together a sequence of stations that address Paul's minute weaknesses. The main goals of his daily training are injury prevention, recovery, flexibility, ankle strength and stability, and hip, core, and glute strength. So far, the approach has yielded impressive returns. "The results have been tremendous since I got here," Paul says. "I didn't believe in lifting weights in high school, because I thought it would mess up my shot. But now I know that it helps me deal with the contact every night. It's not about getting big and bulky; it's about preventing injuries and getting my core strong. Everyone is starting to figure out that's what matters most."

Paul bangs out the following routine, which combines traditional and functional exercises, to make sure his high-speed game is always running smoothly.

FOAM ROLLING

- Place the foam roller between the specified muscle and ground. Roll up and down the entire length of the muscle for 30 seconds. When you locate a sore or tender spot, hold the roller on the spot for a few seconds. Although painful, allow the muscle to relax.

Benefits: Reduced soreness // Myofascial release // Increased flexibility and range of motion

Manson: "We live on the foam rollers here. It's a great way to work out the soreness, keep [the players] loose and fresh, and get them back out on the court feeling better. Chris played a lot of minutes last night, so we have some work to do today."

Cochran: "I find myself telling these guys, 'You're going to love me tomorrow,' when they are doing this. Since it is something unfamiliar, uncomfortable, and slightly painful, they have to trust us that it will work for them."

CP: "This roller finds everything. I am really sore from the game last night, so this is pretty painful. I know it will make me feel better later though."

1. Hamstring
2. IT Band
3. Quad
4. Glute
5. Upper Back
6. Groin

- Perform the following stretches after Foam Rolling. Bring each stretch to a point of tension, then hold for 30 seconds. Repeat on the opposite side when necessary.

Benefits: Injury prevention // Improved flexibility in core, hips, and groin

Manson: "Stretching is one of our main focuses with Chris. He gets pretty tight and sore in his hips and glutes, so that's where we focus."

Cochran: "We have to stay on him about his flexibility. It isn't necessarily a problem, but it could become one if it's overlooked."

CP: "I'm definitely not one of the most flexible guys out there to begin with, and my hips get really tight after games. I have to work on this stuff almost every day."

1. **Seated Hamstring**
2. **Assisted Spinal Twist**
3. **Assisted Lying Spinal Twist**
4. **Assisted Figure 4**

STRENGTH TRAINING

SINGLE-LEG BOSU TOUCH

Manson: "We are trying to improve balance and strengthen the hips and ankles with this. That is all linked together—if there is a problem with one thing, it affects the others. Toward the end of the season, some of the guys suffer from ligament laxity in their ankles—David West could barely push his foot into my hand by the end of last season. So protecting and strengthening their ankles is a big goal for us. We can't prevent a guy from stepping on someone's foot and rolling his ankle, but we can affect how the ankle reacts. We can limit the damage by making those ankles as strong as possible."

Cochran: "Our strength focus is on legs, core, and shoulders. During the season, you have to work your legs whenever you can. It's tough because they are doing so much running, but any time we can get in here and do some leg work, we make sure to get it done."

- Position Bosu so that plastic disc is down

- Balance on left leg on center of Bosu

- Lower into quarter squat and touch right foot to ground in front of Bosu; repeat 5 times

- Touch right foot to ground on right side of Bosu 5 times

- Touch right foot to ground behind Bosu 5 times

- Repeat sequence on right leg

Benefits: Balance // Hip, glute, ankle, and core strength // Hip and ankle stability

2 BOSU CIRCLES

Manson: "The core has to be worked in many different planes—not just uni-dimensionally—so that it can stabilize the spine and work together functionally. Your core needs to be prepared for movement in all directions. Basketball players are like ballerinas with a ball, they are moving and jumping every which way."

- Position Bosu so that plastic disc is up

- Assume athletic stance on plastic disc

- Maintaining balance, use core, hips, and ankles to rotate Bosu clockwise, keeping edge of plastic disc close to ground

- Repeat in counter-clockwise fashion

Benefits: Balance // Hip, glute, and core strength // Hip and ankle stability

3 CHIN-UPS

Cochran: "This is the same motion and uses the same muscles as when you go up and grab the rim to throw down a dunk. It's also similar to going up and fighting for a rebound, which is why you'll hear me yelling, 'Get every rebound! No jump balls!' when they are doing chin-ups."

- Grasp chin-up bar with underhand grip

- Pull body up until chin is above bar

- Lower with control until arms are straight; repeat

Benefits: Upper-body strength // Ball security

4 ALTERNATING DUMBBELL INCLINE

Manson: "We like to superset a lot of things—we pair a primary muscle with the antagonist muscle. That means we alternate push and pull movements. So after we pull with the chin-ups, we go right away to the push with the dumbbell incline."

Cochran: "When we pair the push and pull exercises, the guys keep moving just like on the court. They are pushing and pulling on each other, then they go up for a shot or dunk, and then they have to run. They never stop."

- Position body on incline bench and hold dumbbells at shoulder level

- Drive right dumbbell toward ceiling until arm is straight

- Lower with control; repeat with left arm

- Repeat in alternating fashion

Benefits: Upper-body strength

CHRIS PAUL'S TRAINING GUIDE

EXERCISE		
Foam Rolling	**Sets**	**Seconds**
Hamstring	1	30
IT Band	1	30
Quad	1	30
Glute	1	30
Upper Back	1	30
Groin	1	30

Flexibility	**Sets**	**Seconds**
Seated Hamstring	1 each side	30
Assisted Spinal Twist	1 each side	30
Assisted Lying Spinal Twist	1 each side	30
Assisted Figure 4	1 each side	30

Strength Training	**Sets**	**Reps**
Single-Leg Bosu Touch	2	5 + 5 + 5
Bosu Circles	2	10 each way
Chin-Ups	2	Maximum
Alternating Dumbbell Incline	2	10 each arm

CHAPTER 8

KEVIN DURANT

EDITOR'S NOTE

Strength is hardly the first thing that comes to mind when Kevin Durant's name or game is mentioned. At his NBA Pre-Draft Workout, Durant was pinned under 185 pounds in the bench press test. And even though he's one of the top NBA scorers and a future All-Star, his skinny frame still defines him. Nevertheless, insiders realize how much he's improved since he first took to the hardwood. We knew Durant had been working hard to add muscle [he's bulked up considerably over the past few seasons and can now toss around 185 easily], and that his potential is downright scary considering how much growth lies ahead of him.

Our time with Durant revealed just how lucky he has been over the past few years from a training standpoint. He has worked with some of the best at each level in which he's competed. While Durant played for Montrose Christian, legendary basketball workout guru Alan Stein trained him. During his one year at Texas, Durant worked with Todd Wright, one of the most respected experts in college hoops. And now, as a member of the Oklahoma City Thunder, Durant hands himself over to Dwight Daub, a 10-plus-year NBA S+C veteran whose methods are tried and true.

KEVIN DURANT'S BODY IS LONG AND LANKY, BUT THAT'S NOT BECAUSE HE DOESN'T TRAIN HARD. DURANT'S TRAINING HELPED ELEVATE HIM TO THE NO. 2 PICK IN THE NBA DRAFT.

Likewise, we were lucky to get access to Durant and all three of these training experts. The result was perhaps our most encompassing cover feature to date, highlighting Durant's entire training existence—from gangly teenager to NBA scoring threat. The workout we watched Durant attack with Daub consisted of the stability, flexibility, and strength exercises that have helped Durant add some muscle and mobility to his always-smooth game.

After our meeting, Durant went on to turn heads throughout the 2008-09 NBA season by averaging 25.3 points and 6.5 boards, leading the Thunder out of the NBA cellar, and providing OKC with hope for big things to come.

This is the Kevin Durant cover feature as it originally appeared in the January/February 2009 issue of *STACK* Magazine.

ON THE REBOUND

The Oklahoma City Thunder hadn't won many games. And our visit with the upstart team took place the day after an especially crushing defeat to the Memphis Grizzlies, in a game during which the Thunder flexed a substantial lead throughout only to lose in the waning minutes of play.

We expected to be met with gloom and doom at the team's temporary practice facility, a converted roller rink with corner walls and concession stand still intact. But no moping was evident. In fact, it seemed like the team's psyche was upbeat and positive—enough so that we were tempted to ask the players if they knew they were sporting the NBA's worst record.

Luckily, before asking such a question, everything became clear. This team is full of life and hope in the form of one huge, ever-intensifying bright spot: Kevin Durant.

"I truly see great things ahead for us," Durant says, explaining his team's unexpected attitude. "We work so hard, and guys believe in each other. If we continue to do that, I think the future looks bright for us. We all have a feeling that good times are ahead of us. It's tough that we aren't winning as much as we want, but we'll keep working. This has been my dream since I was six years old. I know there is a long road ahead."

After spending time with the Thunder and watching the 2007–08 NBA Rookie of the Year attack a workout, it was easy to believe in Durant and his team.

"Hard work beats talent when talent fails to work hard." At least according to Durant's godfather, who sat him down to write this inspirational tagline 300 times on a sheet of paper when Durant was 10. And the lesson survived. "This NBA life might be a little hectic," Durant says with a smile. "You might have a good game and think it's going to be like that for the rest of the year, but it's not. That taught me to always make sure that no matter how good I get, I continue to work hard and keep getting better."

Until his godfather's repetitive drill, Durant got by on being the tallest kid on the court and beating everyone down the floor for lay-ups. "I played center," he says, "and I was like a deer running up and down the floor. Since then, I've tried to become more of an athletic player and play above the rim. Once I started working hard and developing those skills, I became more of an athlete."

Durant's hard work shaped him into a lanky, dominant force on the AAU circuit and for basketball powerhouse Oak Hill Academy. "That's how I got known and began to get noticed by college coaches," he recalls. "I got better and became known as a guy who was 6'10" and could dribble and shoot the basketball." However, it wasn't until Kevin met the first of three very important training influences that he really began to develop.

The First Step

Enter Alan Stein, strength and conditioning coach at Montrose Christian. "I met Alan when I was a junior at Oak Hill Academy," Durant says. "He worked with a lot of the elite basketball players in our area, and he told me that I needed to work out with him. I did it one day, and it was tough, but I continued to do it and get better."

After their introduction, Stein began driving an hour each day to pick up Durant, take him to a gym and provide legitimate, structured strength and conditioning sessions. The summer after his junior year, Durant transferred to Montrose Christian, a program his family thought was better suited to his academic and athletic needs.

Scenery wasn't the only difference when Durant switched high schools. As Stein worked

with the young baller throughout his senior year, Durant's body started transforming within weeks. "During our time together, KD put on approximately 25 pounds of muscular body weight," Stein says. "He went from about 180 to 205 by the time he left for college. He drastically increased overall strength in his legs, hips, core, and upper body."

Stein's goals for Durant included reducing the occurrence of injury and improving his on-court performance by strengthening his major muscle groups, using different training modalities [e.g., dumbbells, bodyweight, manual resistance, tubing], teaching work ethic,

and building confidence. It worked. "[Alan] was a very influential person in my life for those two or three years," Durant says. "I got a lot bigger, and he helped me on and off the court. I still do the things he tells me to this day."

A Year to Remember

Durant's year of hardcore training was one key to success when he took his game to Texas. Combined with the Longhorns' perfect environment for improvement, it dramatically accelerated Durant's athletic ability, basketball skills, and maturity in one short season. "I learned a lot just being around my strength coach and basketball coaches every day," Durant says. "They taught me a lot about being a man; I was a long way from home and grew up a lot there. They preached work ethic every day."

Under the watchful eye of Texas basketball strength and conditioning coach Todd Wright, the second training influence in Durant's life, he got even quicker, stronger, more flexible, and bigger. "Todd was a great person for me there," Durant says. "He's one of the reasons I picked Texas. He knows a lot about the body and always made sure we were healthy."

Wright conducted a functional movement screen on Durant during his recruiting trip. Immediately, he determined that the best course of action for Durant was to create a foundation of more mobility in his feet, hips, and thoracic spine [from near the belly button to chest level]. "We felt this would be very important for him to stay healthy in the long run and improve his performance," Wright says. "Kevin still needed to get bigger and stronger, but we first focused on giving him mobility and efficient transfer of energy through his body."

Once Durant's mobility and flexibility were addressed, Wright moved him on to more traditional strength training to build his strength

and size. "I became a lot more flexible, which in turn made me more athletic," Durant boasts. "When I got there, I was about 200 pounds; by the end of the season, I was about 215. We did a great job of working every day."

The improvements paid huge dividends throughout one of the most prolific single seasons in college basketball history. As a freshman, Durant scored double-digits in every game he played, including 20 points or more 30 times and 30 points or more 11 times. He hit 40 percent from behind the arc and averaged 11.1 boards per game—all more than enough to support his decision to jump to the NBA.

Despite all of his accomplishments, Durant's less-than-impressive upper-body strength—made famous by basketball analysts who apparently don't understand the physics or demands of basketball—was exposed during the NBA Pre-Draft Bench test. "A lot of people talked about me not being able to bench press 185, but that didn't mean much to me, because it didn't have to do much with basketball," Durant says. "And I knew I was getting bigger, stronger, and quicker."

When the people who mattered recognized Durant's more important attributes—athletic and basketball ability—they drafted him second overall in the 2007 NBA Draft.

Seamless in Seattle

In his first taste of NBA ball, with the Sonics, Durant made defenses look silly with 20.3 points per game, shooting a toasty 43 percent from three-point land. His rookie explosion earned him the NBA Rookie of the Year Award. "I'm not real big on awards, but that meant a lot," Durant says. "It was a great stepping stone for me. All the great players have won that award, guys like LeBron James and Chris Paul. I'd rather win more games, but

being named Rookie of the Year at the highest level of basketball is big time."

Despite posting amazing numbers and taking home awards, Durant kept his focus when his team relocated to Oklahoma City. And, with help from Dwight Daub, the Thunder's director of athletic performance and the third major influence in his training saga, Durant learned how much more he can get from his body. "I knew I needed to get bigger, stronger, faster, and more flexible," he says. "I did just that, and I know I can bench 185 pounds now for sure! [laughs] Dwight takes a lot of information from the past coaches I've worked with and incorporates that into his workouts. He's very intense. We work hard every day, whether it's in the weight room or on the court."

By putting him in unstable environments to challenge his central nervous system, Daub has improved Durant's overall strength, balance, and proprioception [body awareness in movement], which together translate into making him an even more dominant force on the court. "Obviously, he's a tremendously gifted athlete and a tremendously gifted basketball player," Daub says. "The past year and past summer, he's done a great job as far as improving from when he first came in. The one thing that is evident is when he finishes around the basket. Now, he's able to keep his feet more ready. Last year, he was always getting knocked to the ground, [ending] up on the floor. He's improved [on that] because of his strength and balance improvements."

As the second-year phenom gets closer to NBA All-Star status, he's still looking to grow. "I want to gain more weight, maybe 10 pounds and keep going from there," Durant says. "I want to be bigger to handle the physical pounding of an 82-game season. On the court, I just want to become a better player and help my team win as much as possible."

Durant's current training regimen is similar to what he was doing with Stein at Montrose Christian. However, Daub has intensified and advanced each exercise to make it more challenging and match Durant's recent development.

TEXAS MOBILITY TRAINING

Here are a few exercises Durant used during his time at Texas to increase flexibility and mobility through his spine, hips, and feet.

THORACIC SPINE EXTENSION

- Position body inside Tru Stretch Cage or under reachable pull-up bar

- Grab top bar with right hand and stabilize body with left hand on side of structure

- Keeping hips even and without leaning excessively to one side, allow spine to extend into stretch

- Hold for specified duration

ROTATIONAL MED BALL THROWS

- Assume athletic stance with wall to left; hold med ball in front

- Rotate right slightly to load right leg and hip

- Explode left, rotating hips to throw ball at wall as hard as possible

- Repeat for specified reps

- Perform set on opposite side

SPLIT-STANCE OVERHEAD CORE MATRIX

Forward:
- Assume split stance with cable machine behind

- Hold cable attachment above head and lean forward slightly to create stretch through abdominal region

- Shift hips back and drive torso forward until it is parallel to ground

- Return to start position with control and repeat for specified reps

- Perform set with opposite leg forward

Rotational:
- Assume split stance with right leg forward and cable machine behind

- Hold cable attachment above right shoulder and lean forward slightly to create stretch and rotation through abdominal region

- Shift hips back and drive torso forward until it is parallel to ground

- Return to start position with control; repeat for specified reps

- Perform set with left leg forward starting over left shoulder

Lateral:
- Assume athletic stance with cable machine to left and hold cable attachment above head

- Shift hips left and drive torso right

- Return to start position with control; repeat for specified reps

- Perform set with cable machine to right

Daub: "I keep my hand on Kevin's knee to make sure there is no [forward] shifting, which can put undue stress on the [knee]. We do a lot of multi-planar movements to place him in a very difficult situation as far as his knee, hip, and back alignment is concerned. This trains him to pull himself out of a position like that when he gets knocked off balance in a game. It's all about strengthening within the different planes that he's going to be involved with in basketball. This trains the true core—rather than just doing an ab exercise like a sit-up."

- Assume athletic stance holding med ball in front

- Keeping shoulders facing straight ahead, step forward and 45 degrees left onto Core Board with right leg

- Lower into crossover lunge position until back knee is just above floor

- Drive backward off right heel into start position

- Perform lunge straight ahead onto Core Board with right leg; return to start position

- Perform lunge forward and 45 degrees right onto Core Board with right leg, return to start position

- Repeat sequence for specified reps

- Perform set with left leg

COACHING POINTS

- ➥ Keep lunging knee behind toes
- ➥ Draw stomach in throughout set
- ➥ Keep shoulders straight ahead, not in direction you're stepping

Basic — Med Ball Multi-Planar Lunge: Perform same exercise without Core Boards

Stein: "This is used to vary the normal front-to-back range of motion as well as strengthen the muscles of the groin and hips."

THREE-WAY MED BALL SINGLE-LEG RDL ON AIREX PAD

Daub: "This isolates the hamstring and glute because of the stabilization factor. It's also a tremendous exercise for ankle stabilization when you introduce the Airex Pad."

- Standing on one leg on Airex Pad, hold med ball in front

- Keeping back flat, shoulder blades together, and balancing leg slightly bent, fold at waist and bring med ball toward one of three cones set up in front of you

- Return to start position; perform movement to each of other two cones

- Repeat for specified reps

- Perform set on opposite leg

Basic — Med Ball Single-Leg RDL:
Perform exercise with foot on flat ground.

Stein: "This strengthens the [back] side of the body and works the stabilizing muscles, tendons, and ligaments of the ankle, knee, and hip."

COACHING POINTS

- ➧ Keep back flat
- ➧ Don't allow knee to shift forward
- ➧ Keep back leg straight behind you

Daub: "This is great for single-leg proprioception and balance. It is a combo lift because it's a bicep curl associated with a shoulder press. Combo exercises allow us to get our training done in less time and also to put Kevin in a position where he has to stabilize with his core to go through the different movements."

- Balance on one leg, holding dumbbells at sides with palms facing forward

- Curl dumbbells to shoulders, then press them straight overhead as you rotate palms to face out

- Slowly lower dumbbells to start position through same movement pattern

- Repeat for specified reps

COACHING POINTS

- ➡ Keep balancing knee slightly bent
- ➡ Don't swing dumbbells
- ➡ Don't overarch back during press

Basic — Dumbbell Overhead Press:
Perform Press with dumbbells while standing on both feet

Stein: "This strengthens the shoulders and core. I prefer to use the standing position to involve all of the body's stabilizing muscles."

INVERTED ROW ON PHYSIOBALL

WITH TRX STRAPS OR SUSPENSION

Daub: "The ball adds another dimension that makes it more difficult. It becomes a core exercise because he has to stabilize his entire body in a straight line, and he is still getting the rowing effect of the exercise."

- Hold onto straps, then place heels on top of physioball, making sure body is in straight line

- Keeping body rigid, pull body up until chest is even with hands

- Lower with control until arms are straight

- Repeat for specified reps

Basic — Inverted Row:
Perform exercise holding onto barbell with feet on ground

Stein: "This strengthens the posterior side of the body and is a nice alternative for players who have difficulty doing standard pull-ups."

COACHING POINTS

➥ **Equally distribute weight with feet on ball**
➥ **Keep body straight with no sag in hips**
➥ **Get full extension with arms at bottom of movement**

Daub: "This is a tremendous combination exercise that trains the entire upper body. You use your shoulders, lats, chest, and core for stabilization. The reps depend on the strength level of the athlete. It's not easy!"

- Assume push-up position with light dumbbells in hands and legs slightly wider than hip width

- Walk left dumbbell forward a few inches, then right dumbbell while dragging legs forward

- Perform push-up

- Perform row with left arm, then right

- Repeat sequence [walk, walk, push-up, row, row] for specified reps

COACHING POINTS

- ➡ Keep opposite arm locked out during row
- ➡ Keep body in straight line
- ➡ Keep feet wide to help balance

Basic — Dumbbell Row from Push-Up Position: Perform rows in alternating fashion without walking the dumbbells forward or performing push-ups

Stein: "This is a tremendous exercise when you have limited equipment. It strengthens all muscles of the upper body."

KEVIN DURANT'S TRAINING GUIDE

EXERCISE	Sets	Reps
Thoracic Spine Extension	2	30 seconds each side
Rotational Med Ball Throws	3	8 each side
Split-Stance Overhead Core Matrix [Forward, Rotational, Lateral]	2	10 each variation
Note: Exercises above are from Durant's Texas workout	4	6
Med Ball Multi-Planar Lunge on Core Board	2-4	9-12 each leg
OR Med Ball Multi-Planar Lunge	2-4	9-12 each leg
Three-Way Med Ball Single-Leg RDL on Airex Pad	2-4	5-7 each leg
OR Med Ball Single-Leg RDL	2-4	5-7 each leg
Single-Leg Dumbbell Curl-to-Press	3	4-6-8 [switch legs halfway through each set]
OR Dumbbell Overhead Press	3	4-6-8 [switch legs halfway through each set]
Inverted Row on Physioball With TRX Straps	3-4	6-10
OR Inverted Row	3-4	6-10
Walking Dumbbell Push-Up-to-Row	2-4	3-8 [entire sequence constitutes one rep]
OR Dumbbell Row from Push-Up-Position	2-4	3-8 [entire sequence constitutes one rep]
Note: Exercise in light blue rows is basic version of exercise directly above it		

CHAPTER 9

JERMAINE
O'NEAL

EDITOR'S NOTE

Jermaine O'Neal was an obvious selection as a *STACK* cover athlete. He went straight from high school to the pros, became a dominant force in the NBA and made regular mid-winter appearances as an Eastern Conference All-Star. So when Indiana Pacers strength and conditioning coach Shawn Windle called us about featuring O'Neal, we quickly agreed.

But when we caught up with O'Neal during the summer of 2006, he was one frustrated dude. Heading into his 11th NBA season, the 6'11" forward-center had been dealing with a string of recent injuries. No broken bones or blown-out knees—just strained shoulders and other nagging afflictions, all of which had limited O'Neal's previously explosive play on the hardwood. Simply put, his game was flat.

Windle was working to inject some lift back into O'Neal's game by helping him channel his frustration into hard work and effective training. O'Neal's workouts consisted of various stability and strengthening exercises aimed at helping him slim down, stay healthy, and regain his youthful quicks and hops.

EFFECTIVE TRAINING HAS HELPED JERMAINE O'NEAL, SHOWN BATTLING FOR POSITION AGAINST THE JAZZ, REINVIGORATE HIS GAME.

Windle's functional training, which was new to O'Neal as he was mostly used to non-functional exercises like leg extensions, produced serious benefits. During the 2006–07 season, he started 69 games for the Pacers, compared with only 47 and 41 during his previous two campaigns. He also tossed in nearly 20 points per game while increasing his averages in both blocked shots and rebounds.

Since then, O'Neal has played for the Toronto Raptors and Miami Heat. Despite the bouncing around, he has continued to post respectable numbers toward the end of a very productive career, highlighted by his Pacers franchise records—for most blocks in a game [10], most blocks in a season [228], most rebounds in a playoff game [22], highest rebounding average in a playoff series [17.5], and most free throws attempted in a game [25].

This is the Jermaine O'Neal cover feature as it originally appeared in the November 2006 issue of *STACK* Magazine.

THE RESURRECTION

I have to remind myself of the physical and mental resurrection that's possible each year. Whether I'm dealing with setbacks, injuries, or off-court issues from the year before, the beginning of each year is a chance for me to resurrect myself. I need to come back better than I was the year before. I've always got to be improving. That's why it's written on my shoulder, to remind me every day. —Jermaine O'Neal

Jermaine O'Neal spent his early years wowing crowds in Columbia, South Carolina, with his athleticism on the hardwood and blacktop. Although tall and lanky as a preteen, he possessed speed, quickness, and jumping ability that put his game way beyond others of his age.

A natural lefty, O'Neal was a force driving to and scoring on that side. In grade school, though, he broke his left wrist. It was a hindrance at first, but his cast became a blessing in disguise. O'Neal's mother Angela taught him how to write with his right hand, and he soon became completely capable with it. A few months later, a fully healed O'Neal returned to the court with a reinvented, ambidextrous game.

At the age of 14, a 6'4" O'Neal brought his double-threat skills to Eau Claire High School. With his ability to drain threes, run the break, and beat defenders to the hole, he played the guard position with flair and success.

In his sophomore year, the young phenom experienced a five-inch growth spurt, which affected his court presence dramatically. While maintaining the coordination and speed of a guard, O'Neal became a dominant rebounder and defender in the paint. His new body, new role, and dazzling play led Eau Claire to its third straight division 3A state title.

When he was 16, O'Neal jumped on the opportunity to capture the recruiting spotlight from better-known prospects. At an ABCD summer camp, in front of an audience of college coaches, he dominated Tim Thomas, the nation's top prep star. Further solidifying his status as a top recruit, he posted an impressive senior season, averaging 22.5 points, 12.4 rebounds, and 5.2 blocks. These big numbers earned him All-State First Team honors, the title of South Carolina's "Mr. Basketball," and a spot in the McDonald's All-America Game. Phone calls and visits from coaches became a frequent thing for the high-profile recruit.

Shaky grades, however, jeopardized O'Neal's college eligibility. So, he changed course and set his sights on the NBA. Although some advised against it, O'Neal looked at his ability to hold his own against fellow South Carolinian and NBA rising star Kevin Garnett, and convinced himself that he had what was necessary to make the jump.

Confirming O'Neal's self-assessment, the Portland Trail Blazers took him as the 17th overall pick in the 1996 NBA Draft. As he grew into the NBA game, O'Neal charted a few unspectacular seasons with the Blazers; in 2000, he was dealt to the Indiana Pacers in exchange for Dale Davis.

Finding a better fit with Indy, O'Neal became a different player from the first day. In his first season with the Pacers, he tripled his scoring and rebounding averages; in his second year, he jumped to 19 points and 10.5 boards, earning the NBA's Most Improved Player Award. Over the next few seasons, he averaged enough high-digit double-doubles to put him in the exclusive 20-10 club.

Although his stats and performance remain elite by anyone's measure, O'Neal's recent injuries have slowed his ascension—and, therefore, the Pacers' pursuit of a championship. "Injuries have been my Achilles heel recently," he says. "I hurt my shoulder on a freak play. Someone grabbed my arm as I was going up for a dunk. Things like that really wear on you." His frustration—exacerbated by postseason disappointments—has set the stage for another O'Neal-style revival.

"At times I feel like packing it in, but the motivation from my family pushes me through. They are the biggest source of inspiration in my life," O'Neal says. "I am rededicating and refocusing myself, because I want my kids to be able to live a certain way. They are going to see me working hard and challenging myself, so they will know how to do it, too."

O'Neal's resurgence got the impetus it needed in June. "This was the first summer that I was healthy enough to not wait until August or September to start my training," he says. "Two weeks after we lost, I was back in the weight room getting my body ready for this year."

Gone are his trademark cornrows and nagging injuries of the past; it's a brand-new season for the Pacers' big man. "I feel like I took a step back last year," he says. "But I'm getting back to my original high level this year to make an MVP run. And I'm going to get my team back on top."

Back on Top

In 2005, shortly after joining the Pacers as head strength and conditioning coach, Shawn Windle accepted responsibility for helping O'Neal revive his body and game. "When I got here, Jermaine was hesitant about working with me," Windle says. "He was doing his own thing—a lot of upper body work and exercises like leg extensions. Then one day, he came to me and said, 'Let me see what you can do.' So I worked him out, and he couldn't walk for a few days. He knew it was going to be good for him, though. Since then, he's handed his body over to us and dedicated himself to getting back to where he was."

Recalling his introduction to Windle, O'Neal says: "I didn't do any sort of training in high school—but I wish I did. Even after I got to the NBA, I usually just worked my arms and shoulders. Shawn really changed things up for me. I knew his stuff was good when I started getting sore in my legs, core, and other areas that never got sore."

To put O'Neal's game back on top, Windle crafted a plan to streamline the big man's 6'11" frame. "Jermaine is very big and strong on top because of the upper-body work he was doing," Windle says. "He's gotten a lot bigger in recent years, which got him away from the athletic game for which he was known. He turned into a real banger. Last year, he was 266 pounds. We're trying to get him to 250 to help him get back his lift, explosiveness, and quickness."

O'Neal's work with Windle has already resulted in big gains for the perennial Eastern Conference All-Star. "I've lost 11 pounds this off-season and have got a lot of my quickness back on the court," he boasts. Windle's emphasis on functional core, hip, glute, and leg training is the catalyst for this early success. "All of these things will prevent future injuries, increase his conditioning, and improve his movement," Windle says.

Check out the training O'Neal has been using twice a week to shape his resurrection.

©AP Images

GLUTE ACTIVATION AND CORE STABILITY

O'Neal has improved strength and stability in his hips, low back, and abdominals with this routine. When performing it, Windle suggests thinking of your body as a flat tabletop that nothing can roll off. Keep your hips high and make sure your pelvis isn't rotating at all.

1 BRIDGE

- Lie on back with knees bent and feet flat on ground

- Form straight line from shoulders to knees by raising body so only feet and shoulder blades touch ground; hold

2 PLANK

- Lie on stomach with elbows bent beneath you

- Keeping body in straight line, raise onto forearms and toes; hold

3 PLANK WITH LEG RAISE

- Assume raised plank position

- Keeping body in straight line, raise left leg 12 inches off floor

- Lower left leg; raise right leg

- Repeat pattern for specified reps

4 BRIDGE WITH LEG EXTENSION

- Assume raised bridge position

- Lift right leg and straighten it

- Lower right leg; raise and straighten left leg

- Continue alternating for specified reps

5 HIGH PLANK WITH FOREARM TOUCH

- Assume push-up position with hips in line with shoulders and knees

- Lift left hand; touch it to right forearm

- Lower left hand to floor; repeat with right hand

- Continue alternating for specified reps

6 BRIDGE WITH LEG ROTATION

- Assume raised bridge position

- Raise left leg a few inches; rotate it outward so left foot touches right knee

- Lower left leg; raise and repeat rotation with right leg

- Continue alternating for specified reps

7 PHYSIOBALL PLANK WITH KNEE RAISE

- Assume plank position with feet on ground and hands on center of physioball

- Keeping body in straight line, pull right knee toward chest

- Place right foot back on ground; repeat with left knee

- Continue alternating for specified reps

RESISTANCE TRAINING

ANKLE BAND SHUFFLE

- Loop ankle band around toes of each foot

- Assume balanced stance with knees slightly bent

- Slowly shuffle to right for specified reps

- Repeat to left

Benefits: Strengthens abductors and gluteus medius, a common weak spot for basketball players // Strengthens ankles because the band is around your toes

SINGLE-ARM SPLIT-SQUAT TO PRESS

- Place end of barbell in corner of room

- Face corner and assume lunge position with left leg forward; hold other end of bar with right hand at shoulder level

- Maintaining stable base, quickly drive bar up and out until arm is straight

- Perform specified reps; then repeat with right leg forward and left arm pressing

COACHING POINTS

➧ Do not allow shoulders to twist
➧ Keep base stable
➧ Be quick and light with the press

Benefits: Lunge position works leg strength, because you're in a functional position // Unstable stance works your core and balance

SINGLE-ARM SPLIT-SQUAT TO ROW

• Face cable machine in lunge position with left leg forward

• Hold handle from low position with right hand

• Quickly rotate right, pull handle toward chest, then raise handle up and slightly right

• Return to start position; repeat for specified reps

• Perform on other side

Benefits: Row portion works trunk stability and rotational strength, because you're keeping your upper body stable when you pull

4 SINGLE-LEG SQUAT TO BOX

- Place knee-high box behind you

- Balancing on right leg, slowly sit back into squat until butt touches box

- Rise up and forward into start position

- Repeat with left leg

Benefits: Single-leg strength and balance

COACHING POINTS

➡ Lower with control; do not drop down
➡ Sit back so that the squatting knee does not go over your toes

5 PHYSIOBALL LEG CURL

- Lie on back with feet on physioball

- Raise body into straight line so that only shoulder blades touch floor

- Keeping hips high, curl ball toward butt

- Slowly allow ball to roll back out until legs are straight

Benefits: Lower back, glute, and hamstring strength.

COACHING POINTS

➡ Keep your hips above your heels the whole time
➡ Keep your body in straight line

JERMAINE O'NEAL'S TRAINING GUIDE

GLUTE ACTIVATION AND CORE STABILITY

Exercise	Sets/Reps or Duration
Bridge	1 X 30 seconds
Plank	1 X 30 seconds
Plank with Leg Raise	1 X 6 each leg
Bridge with Leg Extension	1 X 6 each leg
High Plank with Forearm Touch	1 X 6 each leg
Bridge with Leg Rotation	1 X 6 each leg
Physioball Plank with Knee Raise	1 X 6 each leg

RESISTANCE TRAINING

Exercise	Sets/Reps
Ankle Band Shuffle	3 X 10 each direction
Single-Arm Split-Squat to Press	3 X 10 each side
Single-Arm Split-Squat to Row	3 X 10 each side
Single-Leg Squat to Box	2 X 8 each leg
Physioball Leg Curl	2 X 10

CHAPTER '10

CARMELO ANTHONY

WITH KENYON MARTIN

EDITOR'S NOTE

We first encountered Carmelo Anthony during his second season in the NBA. In 2003, as a freshman in college, he led Syracuse to a 30–5 record and the school's first NCAA championship. Picked third overall in the 2003 NBA Draft, Anthony made himself known throughout the NBA during his rookie year. But in terms of strength and conditioning, the young Nugget was just getting into it. Anthony had a lot to learn from Nuggets strength coach and industry leader Steve Hess.

Hess was eager to introduce Anthony to his style of basketball training, and he was all over Anthony from the moment the Nuggets drafted him. Hess' goal was to enhance the young phenom's raw athleticism while leaning out and toning up Anthony's somewhat soft body. The means consisted of a customized cardio-packed, multi-joint training routine and a strict eating plan—something that the college Anthony wouldn't have known about if Hess had snatched the cheeseburger out of his hand. Anthony admitted that before joining Denver, his training consisted of hooping and his diet consisted of frequent runs to the nearest Wendy's.

CARMELO ANTHONY BRINGS THE BALL UP COURT FOR THE NUGGETS. AS HE TRANSITIONED TO THE NBA, ANTHONY IMPROVED HIS DIET AS WELL AS HIS EXERCISE REGIMEN.

Without even glancing at a stat sheet, we noted the obvious results of Anthony's work with Hess. Lean, defined muscles had popped up where Anthony's self-described "baby fat" had once resided. Quickness, explosion, and late-game endurance had become new weapons for the dominant forward. As for the stat sheet: during his third season, Anthony's scoring average hopped up nearly six points to 26.5, and it climbed even higher to 28.9 the following year.

During his six years in the league, Anthony has established himself as one of the NBA's elite, fit players, a perennial All-Star, and a team leader for the NBA-Championship-contending Nuggets. Over that time, we have sat down with Anthony two additional times to garner updates on his current fitness, training, and nutrition. Each time, Anthony made it clear that what he learned from Hess early in his career is now a way of life. He's still a big fan of Hess and his methods, and he continues to knock out grueling workouts and take down skinless chicken breast on a daily basis.

This is the Carmelo Anthony cover feature as it first appeared in the May 2005 issue of *STACK* Magazine.

SUPERSTAR RECIPES

One Denver Nuggets superstar fights to keep the weight off. Enter the Yin: Carmelo "Melo" Anthony. Another Nuggets superstar battles to maintain his bulk. Enter the Yang: Kenyon "K-Mart" Martin.

Anthony, a small forward, needs explosive speed and agility to remain an offensive threat.

Martin, a power forward, requires strength to dominate the paint as a defensive force.

Anthony reaches his goals using a cardiovascular training component.

Martin achieves his through a strength-training component.

Variation from one Nugget's training goals to another doesn't stop with these two. Check out Denver's reserves. Earl Boykins, the shortest player in the NBA at 5'5", needs to maintain the strength and size gains he's made to stay competitive on the NBA hardwood. Francisco Elson, a seven-foot forward-center, works to pack on pounds to his stretched-out frame. Looking to make his way back on the court altogether, Nene works on rehabbing a sprained left knee.

Every player has individual training goals and a unique body type, but each has one final result in mind—to be the best athlete possible. Helping each player achieve that result is Steve Hess.

Hess, Denver's strength and conditioning coach, tailors each player's core, flexibility, strength, and nutrition program to specific training needs and body type. Even though only a one-inch height difference separates Carmelo Anthony and Kenyon Martin, these two are perfect examples of players who necessitate very different training programs.

Anthony's program focuses on keeping his 6'8", 220-pound frame lean, which can be difficult when dealing with a 20-year-old on a college student's diet. "I love fried foods," he says. "But I can't eat 'em. And I can't eat too many carbohydrates either."

To keep his heavier frame lean, Hess trains Anthony in a circuit format. "Although his reps are low, if you put them all together, it's still a high-rep routine because you're going through it rapidly," Hess explains. "The reps add onto each other since he's never really resting."

Martin has the opposite challenge: keeping his lean frame heavy. "Maintaining my weight has been my biggest challenge," Martin says. "One day, I'll come in around 235 pounds, and the next day I'll show up at 220."

To help him sustain his weight, Hess eliminates a cardiovascular component from Martin's program. "We give him more rest," Hess explains. "I don't want him to lose any weight, so I'm just trying to get to the strength component."

Flexibility also distinguishes each power player. Hess says Martin is slightly more flexible in the hamstring, but Anthony in the quadriceps. "That is why I have Kenyon do quad stuff on the power plate. I've had success with these specific stretching regimens in injury prevention," he says.

Following is a detailed look at just one day of Anthony's and Martin's core, flexibility, and weight-training regimens. The two players' programs change day to day as well as throughout the season, based on playing time, conditioning needs, and injuries.

"I don't do the same workout as Melo and Melo doesn't do the same workout as Andre [Miller]," Martin says. "But that's the beauty of it."

SWISS BALL REVERSE HYPER WITH BANDS

- With small band around ankles, lie on stomach on Swiss Ball with hands and feet on ground

- Raise legs until legs and body form straight line

- Spread legs as far apart as possible

- Bring legs back together; lower to start position

- Repeat for specified reps

COACHING POINTS

- ➤ Raise legs until parallel to ground
- ➤ Keep body as straight as possible
- ➤ Use arms to help maintain balance
- ➤ Point toes to ground
- ➤ Perform slowly and with control

LUMBAR SWISS BALL SUPERMAN

- Lie with stomach on Swiss Ball with hands and feet on ground

- Raise one arm and opposite leg off ground; hold

- Return to start position; perform with opposite arm and leg

COACHING POINTS

➡ Maintain straight line with working arm and leg

➡ Use arm and leg in contact with ground to maintain balance ➡ Perform slowly and with control

LUMBAR BRIDGING

- Lie with shoulder blades on Swiss Ball; place feet flat on ground

- Raise arms above chest

- Lift one foot off ground and extend leg

- Return to start position; perform with opposite leg

COACHING POINTS

➡ At start position, maintain straight line from knees to shoulders

➡ Fully extend arms toward ceiling

➡ Lifted leg should be parallel to ground

➡ Perform slowly and with control

LUMBAR STANDING ROTATION

- Assume athletic stance holding Swiss Ball at chest level with arms fully extended

- Rotate torso left until ball is outside left hip

- Rotate torso right until ball is outside right hip

- Repeat for specified time

COACHING POINTS

➡ Keep arms fully extended and parallel to floor throughout exercise
➡ Keep head forward during movement
➡ Maintain a shoulder-width stance
➡ Perform slowly and with control

ANTHONY — WEIGHTLIFTING

STANDING LAT PULLDOWN WITH BAND ABDUCTION

- With band secured around legs just above knees, assume athletic stance in front of lat pull down machine

- Grasp straight bar attachment with slightly wider than shoulder-width grip

- Squat until thighs are parallel to floor

  - Pull bar down to chest

  - Return to start position

  - Repeat for specified reps

COACHING POINTS

➡ Maintain shoulder-width stance ➡ Keep head up, back flat, and toes pointed forward during exercise
➡ Avoid using body for momentum ➡ Perform movement with control

2. SWISS BALL ALTERNATING DUMBBELL PRESS
[WITH MED BALL BETWEEN KNEES]

- Lie on upper back on Swiss Ball holding dumbbells in hands and med ball between knees

- Fully extend arms toward ceiling

- Lower left dumbbell to chest level; press back to start position

- Perform with opposite arm

- Repeat for specified reps

COACHING POINTS

➡ Maintain straight line from knees to shoulders
➡ While one arm is pressing dumbbell, other arm remains extended
➡ Avoid using body for momentum
➡ Perform with control

3. SINGLE-LEG EXTENSION

- Assume position in leg extension machine

- Extend right leg so it is straight

- Lower weight until leg is back to starting position

- Perform with left leg

- Repeat for specified reps

COACHING POINTS

➡ Keep head up and back flat
➡ Avoid using body for momentum
➡ Perform with control

CARMELO ANTHONY   135

MARTIN — CORE

REVERSE HYPEREXTENSION WITH ABDUCTION

- With small band attached around ankles, lie backward on hyperextension machine or on stomach on top of large box

- Using lower back muscles and glutes, raise legs until they are parallel to floor

- Spread legs as far as possible

- Bring legs back together; lower to start position

- Repeat for specified reps

COACHING POINTS

- ➡ At start position, legs should be hanging off apparatus so body is folded in half at waist
- ➡ Avoid using body for momentum
- ➡ Perform with control

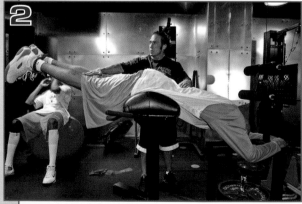

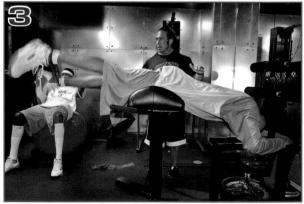

2 SIDE TWIST TOP BOTTOM, BOTTOM TOP

- Assume athletic stance holding med ball in front of body and near waist level

- Raise med ball over left shoulder

- Return to start position; perform to right

- Repeat for specified reps

COACHING POINTS

➡ Keep slightly-wider-than-shoulder-width stance
➡ Keep arms fully extended throughout exercise
➡ Keep core tight and back straight
➡ Go through full range of motion
➡ Perform with control

MARTIN — FLEXIBILITY

HAMSTRING OFF POWER PLATE

- Place right heel on Power Plate, keeping leg straight

- Lean forward and touch toes of right foot with right hand

- Hold for specified time

- Repeat on opposite leg

COACHING POINTS

➡ Maintain slight bend in knee on leg that's off Power Plate
➡ Keep toes pointed toward ceiling

2 QUADRICEPS OFF POWER PLATE

• Assume lunge position with back knee on Power Plate and front foot on floor

• Reach back and grab foot of leg on Power Plate

• Pull foot toward butt and hold for specified time

• Repeat on opposite leg

COACHING POINTS

➤ Keep chest and head up and shoulders back
➤ Keep knee behind toes on front leg

3 HIP FLEXOR OFF POWER PLATE

• Assume lunge position with back knee on Power Plate and front foot on floor

• Take step with front foot for wider lunge than one used with quad stretch

• Lean deeper into position for hip flexor stretch

• Hold for specified time

• Repeat on opposite leg

COACHING POINTS

➤ Keep chest and head up and shoulders back
➤ Leg position should be further than regular lunge

EXTERNAL ROTATIONS

- With cable machine to left, stand on Airex Pad and hold handle set at waist height with right hand

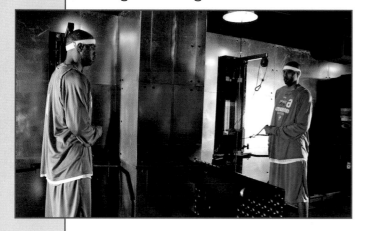

- Bend right arm 90 degrees and position hand near navel

- Rotate arm out and away from body as far as possible

- Return to start position; repeat for specified reps

- Perform with opposite arm for specified reps

COACHING POINTS

➡ Avoid twisting body during movement ➡ Keep elbow tight to body throughout exercise
➡ Perform with control ➡ Go through full range of motion

SINGLE-ARM INCLINE DB PRESS

- Lie on incline bench with dumbbell near chest

- Extend leg opposite of working hand

- Press dumbbell until arm is fully extended

- Lower to start position and repeat for specified reps

- Perform with opposite arm and leg for specified reps

COACHING POINTS

➡ Rest free hand near waist ➡ Avoid using body for momentum
➡ Go through full range of motion ➡ Perform under control

ANTHONY'S EXERCISE SCHEDULE

Time	Description
Pre-Practice	*Core:* prior to every practice *Stretching:* prior to every practice
Post-Practice	*Resistance training:* 3 times per week *Explosive work:* 2 times per week

CORE

Exercise	Weights	Sets	Reps
Swiss Ball Crunch	14-pound med ball	3	20
Reverse Crunch [Ball Between Legs]	7-pound med ball	3	20
Opposite Crunch	7-pound med ball	3	20
Swiss Ball Side Crunch	7-pound med ball	3	20
Swiss Ball Reverse Hyper with Bands	Green Band	3	20
Front Stabilization: Right or Left Side Stabilization	Body weight	3	1 min

Notes: *Don't rest between exercises or sets; complete circuit three times. Drink water throughout.*

FLEXIBILITY

Exercise	Sets/Reps or Duration
Neck Stretch	1/15 seconds
Thoracic Stretch • Flexion • Rotation • Side-Bend	1/15 reps
Lumbar • Swiss Ball Superman • Bridging • Standing Rotation	1/15 seconds
Hamstring	1/15 seconds
Quadriceps	1/15 seconds
IT Band	1/15 seconds
Shoulders • Posterior Shoulder Stretch • Inferior Shoulder Stretch • External Rotation	1/15 seconds

Wrist Flexion/Pronation		1/15 reps
Specific Swiss Ball Stretch • Ball Circle [left and right] • Ball [side to side] • Ball [forward and back]		1/15 reps

Notes: *Move from stretch to stretch without rest.*

Non-Game Day Weightlifting

Exercise	Weights	Sets	Reps
Standing Lat Pulldown with Band Above Knees	8 plates 9 plates 10 plates	3	10 8 6
Swiss Ball Alternating Dumbbell Press [with Med Ball Between Knees]	50 pounds 65 pounds 60 pounds	3	10 8 6
Power One-Arm Row [rapid-fire]	60 pounds 60 pounds 60 pounds	3	6 6 6
Iso Chest Pass	155 pounds 155 pounds 155 pounds	3	6 6 5
Reverse Fly Straight Arm Raise Triceps Kickback [Complex]	12 pounds	3	10 10 10
Dumbbell Curl Press [off pads]	25 pounds 25 pounds 25 pounds	3	6 6 6
Power Plate Squat Power Plate Hold Power Plate Jump	0	3	8
Single-Leg Extension [partial range]	5 plates 5 plates 5 plates	3	45s 45s 45s
Swiss Ball Single-Leg Curl	0	3	8
Calf Raises [standing]	200 pounds 200 pounds 200 pounds	3	30 30 30
Standing Calf Jumps	0 0 0	3	20 20 20

Notes: *Complete full circuit three times through without rest.*

MEAL SCHEDULE

Time	Type of Food	Quantity
8 a.m.	• Oatmeal • Egg Whites • Condiments as desired • Fruit	• 2 cups • 10 • 1 cup • 1
1:30 p.m.	• Balanced Shake • Banana	• 1 serving • 1
3:30 p.m.	• Tuna • Yams • Broccoli • Green apple	• 6 ounces • 8 ounces • 2 cups • 1
5:30 p.m.	• Grilled chicken • Brown rice • Green apple • Almonds	• 8 ounces • 2 cups • 1 • 15
8:30 p.m.	• Salmon • Sweet potato • Vegetables	• 8 ounces • 3 ounces • 2 cups

Notes: *Meals should be eaten within half hour of given times.*
• *Meals should not be eaten within one hour prior to workout.*
• *Meals of high carbohydrate content should be consumed two hours before the workout and immediately after.*
• *Three liters of water should be consumed throughout the day.*
• *Multi vitamin, multi mineral Glucosamine, and Chondroiton sulphate (essential oils, extra calcium, digestive aid) are consumed after three main meals.*

MARTIN'S EXERCISE SCHEDULE

Time	Description
Pre-Practice	*Core:* prior to every practice *Stretching:* prior to every practice
Post-Practice	*Resistance training:* 3 times per week *Specific leg work:* 4 times per week

CORE

Exercise	Weights	Sets	Reps
Reverse Hyperextension with Abduction	Green Band	3	20
Bent Leg Lift With Med Ball Between Legs	7 pounds	3	20
Plyo Med Ball Crunch	7 pounds	3	20
Russian Twist With Throw	7 pounds	3	20
Side Twist Top Bottom, Bottom Top	7 pounds	3	20
Swiss Ball Circles	Body weight	3	20

Notes: *Rest for 30 seconds between exercises and sets.*
Drink water throughout the workout.

FLEXIBILITY

Exercise	Sets/Reps or Duration
Lumbar • Swiss Ball Superman • Bridging • Standing Rotation	1/15 seconds
Hamstring Off Power Plate	1/15 seconds
Quadriceps Off Power Plate	1/15 seconds
Hip Flexor Off Power Plate	1/15 seconds
Shoulders • Posterior Shoulder Stretch • Inferior Shoulder Stretch • External Rotation	1/15 seconds
Specific Swiss Ball Stretches With Green Band Above Knees • Ball Circle [left and right] • Ball [side to side] • Ball [forward and back]	1/15 reps

Notes: *Move from stretch to stretch without rest.*

Non-Game Day Weightlifting Regimen

Exercise	Weights	Sets	Reps
External Rotations	2 plates	3	20 20 20
Power Shrugs	185 pounds 225 pounds 225 pounds	3	6 6 6
Low Cable Rows	10 plates 11 plates 12 plates	3	10 8 6
Single-Arm Incline DB Press	70 pounds 75 pounds 80 pounds	3	8 6 4
Single-Arm High Pull	4 plates 4.5 plates 5 plates	3	10 8 6
Single-Arm DB Press Off One Leg	30 pounds 35 pounds 40 pounds	3	8 6 4
Reverse Fly	25 pounds 25 pounds 25 pounds	3	6 6 6
Single-Leg Press	90 pounds	3	100
Seated Leg Curl	70 pounds	3	10 10 10
Single-Leg Calf Raises	50 pounds 50 pounds 50 pounds	3	12 12 12

Notes: *Rest one minute between exercises and two minutes between sets.*

MEAL SCHEDULE

Time	Type of Food	Quantity
8 a.m.	• Oatmeal • Egg Whites • Whole Eggs • Condiments as desired • Fruit	• 2 cups • 6 • 2 • 1 cup • 1
1:30 p.m.	• Balanced Shake • Banana	• 1 serving • 1
3:30 p.m.	• Grilled chicken • Yams • Broccoli • Green apple	• 6 ounces • 8 ounces • 2 cups • 1
5:30 p.m.	• Grilled turkey • Brown rice • Green apple • Almonds	• 8 ounces • 2 cups • 1 • 15
8:30 p.m.	• Lean steak • Sweet potato • Vegetables	• 8 ounces • 8 ounces • 2 cups

Notes: *Same as Anthony's*

RECOMMENDED RESOURCES

STACK

For the Athlete, By the Athlete

Originally founded as a magazine, STACK has developed into a fully diversified multimedia company providing information and advice on athletic training, nutrition, and sports skills from top professional and collegiate athletes and coaches on the following major brand platforms:

STACK Media is one of the top sports properties on the Internet, with an average of 4 million unique visitors and 100 million page views per month. Combining its editorial content with product and service offerings from several partner sites in a distributed media network, STACK Media has become the acknowledged leader in reaching its audience of active sports participants online.

STACK.com, the digital home for all STACK content and Web-based tools, is one of the Internet's fastest growing sites delivering information exclusively for the active sports community.

STACK TV, an online video platform with eight channels of unique, originally produced videos, delivers the largest library of sports performance video content on the Web.

STACK Magazine, requested by more than 9,000 high school athletic directors, has a circulation of 800,000 and a readership of more than 5 million high school athletes.

MySTACK, a social network and recruiting site that allows athletes to create profiles with their personal information and stats, upload highlight films and photos, and send their profiles to college coaches to take control of the recruiting process.

Eastbay

Eastbay.com

The leading supplier of athletic footwear, apparel, and training gear, Eastbay.com and its direct mail catalog are essential resources for athletes interested in the top brands, including Nike, Reebok, adidas, and others. As marketing partners, STACK and Eastbay share the goal of helping high school and college athletes meet all of their performance needs. Through Eastbay Training Centers, presented by STACK on Eastbay.com, the retailer offers the latest and greatest in sport performance content as well as its traditional product lines.

beRecruited.com

Founded in 2000 by a former collegiate athlete, beRecruited.com provides a platform for high school student-athletes to connect and interact with college coaches across the nation. More than 200,000 registered student-athletes use beRecruited.com to build online profiles and evaluate opportunities to take their game to the next level. STACK creates content to inform high school athletes of the recruiting process, while beRecruited offers an environment in which athletes can apply their skills and knowledge to achieve their recruiting goals.

Varsity Networks, Inc.

varsitynetworks.com

Varsity Networks helps more than 9,000 high schools across the country manage, motivate, and stay connected with their teams. Users are able to post commentary, video, photos, and team stats to the site. The company also distributes content to local and national media outlets to feature on-air or on their websites. Varsity Network's services have value for all members of the high school sports community, including athletic directors, coaches, players, parents, and fans.

iHigh.com

iHigh.com, Inc. offers free services to high schools and student-athletes throughout the United States, allowing them to create and maintain their own branded websites. Through iHigh.com, teams and news organizations are able to post live broadcasts, stories, photos, and videos to their customized team pages. Student-athletes can also set up individual profiles through the social network, myihigh.com. The iHigh site features the first national network of member schools in one comprehensive online destination.

RECRUITING RESOURCES

National Collegiate Athletic Association
ncaa.org
The NCAA's official website houses its Eligibility Center, which provides information and resources for prospective collegiate student-athletes. The NCAA Eligibility Center offers a guide for college-bound student-athletes, lists of approved high school academic requirements, and registration forms. Also available at ncaa.org is information on legislation and governance, statistics, and records for all NCAA sports and a comprehensive library of NCAA publications and journals.

NUTRITION RESOURCES

Gatorade Sports Science Institute [GSSI]
gssiweb.com
GSSI is a research facility dedicated to sharing the latest information about exercise science and sports nutrition. In an effort to expand education about enhancing athletic performance, the Institute provides services and tools for athletes and sports health professionals, and develops state-of-the-art technology used by the nation's principal scientists who are committed to furthering sports nutrition research.

OTHER RESOURCES

Steve Hess
Denver Nuggets
Strength and conditioning coach
nuggets.com

TRX Suspension Trainer
[$150-plus, fitnessanywhere.com]

FORZA Fitness
forzadenver.com

Alan Stein
Montrose Christian School
montrosechristian.org
Stronger Team
strongerteam.com

Cutting Edge Reaction and Quickness Drills [DVD]
A. Stein, USA: Championship Productions [2008]

Alan Stein's Elite Athlete Training [DVD]
A. Stein, USA: Championship Productions [2006]

Alan Stein's Strength & Power Training for Basketball Players [DVD]
A. Stein, USA: Championship Productions [2006]

Alan Stein's Active Warm-up and Core Training for Basketball Players [DVD]
A. Stein, USA: Championship Productions [2006]

Alan Stein: Off-Season Training for Basketball [DVD]
A Stein, USA: Championship Productions [2006]

Alan Stein: Off-Season Workouts for a Championship Basketball Program [DVD]
A. Stein, USA: Championship Productions [2007]

Alan Stein's Explosive Conditioning for Basketball Players [DVD]
A. Stein, USA: Championship Productions [2006]

Alan Stein: In-Season Training for Basketball Players [DVD]
A. Stein, USA: Championship Productions [2007]

ACL Injury Prevention for Female Athletes [DVD]
A. Stein, USA: Championship Productions [2008]

Todd Wright
University of Texas
texassports.com

Basketball For Dummies
R. Phelps, J. Walters, & T. Bourret, Foster City, CA: IDG Books Worldwide [2000]

Dwight Daub, MS, CSCS, PES, CES
Oklahoma City Thunder
nba.com/thunder

Basketball Exercises: Cutting Edge Conditioning Techniques
Dwight Daub & J. Callero, Core [2005]

Shawn Windle

Indiana Pacers
indianapacers.com

Exercises for the Slide Board DVD
Shawn Windle and Brijesh Patel [$30, sbcoachescollege.com]

Ready to Use Warm-Ups DVD
Shawn Windle and Brijesh Patel [$30, sbcoachescollege.com]

101 Agility Ladder Drills DVD
Shawn Windle and Brijesh Patel [$30, sbcoachescollege.com]

Tubing and Bands Exercises DVD [$30, sbcoachescollege.com]

Erik Phillips

Phoenix Suns
phoenixsuns.com
SportXcel
sportxcel.com

SportXCel Youth Performance [www.sportxcel.com]